PREPARING FOR RETIREMENT
A COMPREHENSIVE GUIDE TO FINANCIAL PLANNING

2018 EDITION

By Ryan Glover, CFP®

Published by Tarheel Advisors, LLC

3300 Battleground Ave. Ste. 204

Greensboro NC 27410

Editor – Walter Hinson, CFP®

Co-editor - Dr. Alan Brown

Graphic Artwork – Jane Pinzauti

PREPARING FOR RETIREMENT
A COMPREHENSIVE GUIDE TO FINANCIAL PLANNING

INTRODUCTION

This is an educational text on financial planning, and more specifically, retirement planning. The primary goal of this book is to give adults the working knowledge and tools to successfully navigate their retirement and plan for their future. Regardless of age, income, or social status, everyone can greatly benefit from having a financial plan.

By educating yourself on finances you are endeavoring on what many people find the hardest part of constructing a financial plan—starting one! Studies have shown repeatedly that Americans as a whole are ill prepared for retirement. Amazingly, according to a study by Aetna and the Financial Planning Association, 31% of pre-retirees would prefer to clean the bathroom or pay bills than plan for retirement.

The next nine chapters will not only help you start a financial plan but will also prepare and guide you through the entire retirement planning process. Remember, well constructed financial and retirement planning is a continued process that requires regular updates.

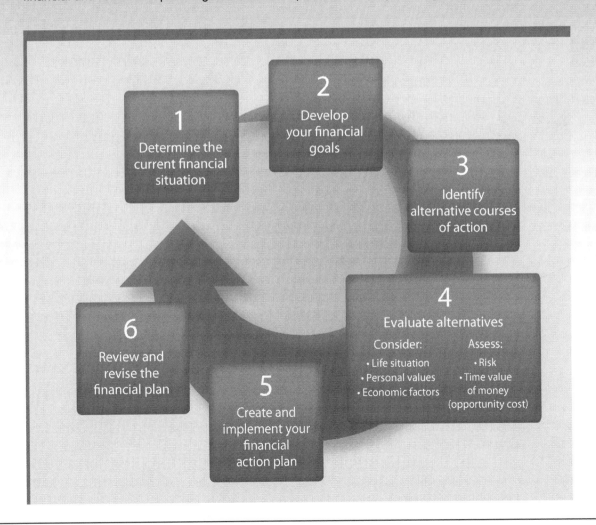

PREPARING FOR RETIREMENT
A COMPREHENSIVE GUIDE TO FINANCIAL PLANNING

CHAPTER 1:

THE PLANNING PROCESS

PREPARING FOR RETIREMENT

A COMPREHENSIVE GUIDE TO FINANCIAL PLANNING

PREPARING FOR RETIREMENT

Many people feel retirement is about figuring out when they want to leave their job, but in reality it is about far more. You may have enough money to leave the workforce, but then what? Retirement planning is about creating a foundation for spending the rest of your life.

With retirement comes the opportunity for extra free time and freedom to relax. However, with this freedom comes a number of questions, such as determining where to spend your time and money.

Remember, you are building the foundation for the rest of your life, which could last for three decades or more. Retirement is not a sprint, so make sure you are preparing yourself for the long haul. You don't want to find yourself bored six months down the road wishing you were back at work.

Build a list of activities you would enjoy in retirement. You could take classes, read, play golf, spend time with family, travel, etc... When considering these activities, also consider the costs associated with them.

KEYS TO PROPER RETIREMENT AND FINANCIAL PLANNING:

– Concentrate on the "process" and don't get stuck on the fine details

– Take financial inventory and understand your assets

– Identify goals and determine which are the most important to you

– Learn key concepts, rates, and terminology

– Create accountability, for yourself and your advisors

– Continued review and updates of your plan

QUESTIONS TO ASK BEFORE RETIREMENT:

– How do you want to spend your free time?

– What activities and hobbies do you enjoy?

– Do you want a second career?

– Are you financially ready?

– Are you emotionally ready?

– Do you want to work in retirement?

– Are you (and your spouse) ready for more time together?

– Do you want to retire at a young age or work longer and have more income?

– Do you want to leave a legacy to your family or charities?

– Are you in good health and have greater longevity in your family?

– Do you want to downsize your home, have a vacation home, or not have a home at all?

– Where do you want to retire?

WHERE YOU RETIRE MATTERS!

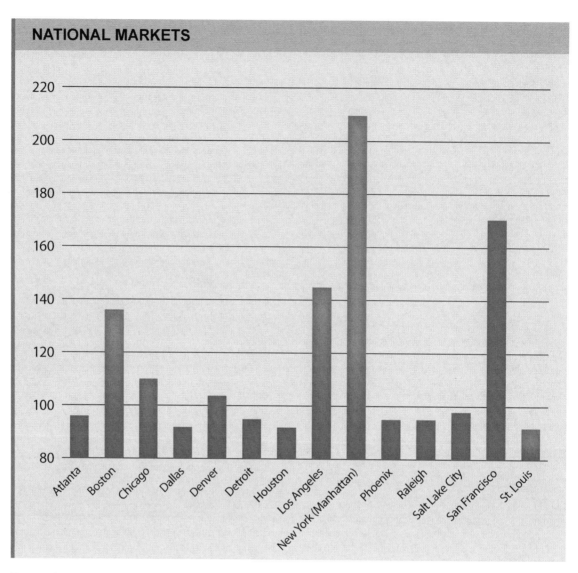

NATIONAL MARKETS

Bureau of Economic Research 2016 Cost of Living Index
100 = National Average

The answers to the prior questions matter for a number of reasons, and the money you'll need to live comfortably in retirement is at the core of many of those questions. For example, the cost of living in different parts of the country (or world) can vary dramatically. Should you decide to live in Manhattan you will need approximately three times the retirement savings as you would for a retirement in Texas.

RETIREMENT & STRESS

According to the Holmes-Rahe Life Stress Inventory survey, retirement is one of the top 10 stressful events individuals will experience. This is no surprise because retirement impacts you socially, emotionally and financially. A well thought out and executed financial plan is one of the best ways of lessening the stress tied to retirement.

Where do your stress levels stand?

Holmes-Rahe Social Readjustment Scale or Life Events Scale

Event	Scale of Impact
Death of Spouse	100
Divorce	73
Marital Separation	65
Jail Term	63
Death of Close Family Member	63
Personal Injury or Illness	53
Marriage	50
Fired at Work	47
Marital Reconciliation	45
Retirement	**45**
Change In Health of Family Member	44
Pregnancy	40
Sex Difficulties	39
Gain of a New Family Member	39
Business Readjustment	39
Change in Financial State	38
Death of Close Friend	37
Change to Different Line of Work	36
Change in Number of Arguments with Spouse	35
Mortgage over $150,000	31
Foreclosure	30
Change in Responsibilities at Work	29
Son or Daughter Leaving Home	29
Trouble with In-Laws	29
Outstanding Personal Achievement	28
Partner Begins or Stops Work	26
Begin or End School	26
Change in Living Conditions	25

KEEPING SCORE

The first step in building a financial plan is to take a financial inventory. Taking inventory is essentially how you keep score and measure where you currently stand financially.

Take inventory of all your assets

Take inventory of all your liabilities

Create a net worth statement.

Develop a Budget

CREATING A NET WORTH STATEMENT

A net worth statement, or personal balance sheet, is a summary of all your assets and liabilities as of some particular date. Simply put, it is a snapshot of your wealth.

To calculate your net worth, you must inventory and value all of your assets and liabilities (worksheet on 10.4). There will be concrete figures for liabilities, but valuing assets may not be quite as easy. Be conservative in valuing assets because overvaluing items will not get you to retirement any faster.

STEPS TO FIGURING NET WORTH

– Label your assets and liabilities

– Fair market value of assets – Be honest! Overvaluing assets won't help you retire faster.

ASSETS TO CONSIDER:

– Personal Residence

– Secondary Residence or Investment Property

– Taxable Investment Accounts

– Bank Accounts

– Cash Value of Insurance Contracts

– Retirement Accounts (IRA, 401(k), Cash Balance Pension Plan, etc.)

– Vehicles

– Personal Property (furniture, jewelry, collectibles)

LIABILITIES TO CONSIDER:

– Mortgage(s)

– Auto Loans

– Student Loan Debt

– Credit Card Debt

– 401(k) Loan

TOTAL ASSETS – TOTAL LIABILITIES = NET WORTH

DEVELOPING A BUDGET

Budgeting is a vital step in the retirement planning process. The reason for its importance is simple; you can't plan for future expenses if you don't know what you're currently spending. Additionally, there are opportunities to identify wasteful spending with close examination. If you're on the borderline of having enough money for retirement, a well-defined budget can be the difference between making your money last or not.

RULE OF THUMB:
In retirement, you can expect to need between 70-90% of your current income to make ends meet.

WHY DO PEOPLE NEED LESS INCOME IN RETIREMENT?

– No retirement plan contributions (Pension, 401(k), 403(b), IRA, etc.)

– FICA taxes (Social Security and Medicare) no longer deducted in retirement

– Lowered work expenses (vehicle and gas costs, lunches out, dry cleaning, etc.)

– Potentially lower tax bracket

CREATING A BUDGET:

– Be honest! – underestimating expenses only hurts yourself

– Monitor 3 to 6 months of spending data

– Evaluate your spending habits

– Modify spending where it is inconsistent with your long-term financial objectives

– Create accountability for your goals

– Don't count on one time occurrences, unrealistic investment returns, or borrowing to fund retirement.

Income (Inflows)	Expenses (Outflows)
Salary, Wages, and Bonuses	Savings (Mutual Funds, IRA, 401(k), etc.)
Interest Income	Taxes (Federal, State, Local, FICA)
Investment Income	Property Taxes
Rental Income	Mortgage or Rent
Business Income	Car Payment and Repairs
Trust Income	Insurance
Pension	Food
Retirement Account Distributions	Utilities
Social Security	Credit Card Payments
Other Income	Health Care, Dental, Prescriptions

INCOME – EXPENSES = NET CASH FLOW

*See page 10-7 for budget worksheet.

LIABILITY MANAGEMENT

Regardless of where you are in life, an equal amount of thought should be put towards managing your liabilities as you spend managing your assets. If you have significant (and growing) debt issues, retirement planning should be secondary in your financial planning efforts. Unless you have substantial assets, borrowing should not be considered a primary source for retirement income.

When it comes to financial planning a home mortgage is of special "interest". For many households a mortgage can account for 1/3 of a family's expenses. So, if you plan on continuing to have a mortgage in retirement you'll need to insure you have the income to support the payments. While cheap and tax deductible interest makes mortgages seem attractive, it is even more attractive to not have to worry about the expense in retirement.

Consider the following:

A $250,000 mortgage at 4.0% costs $1,193.54 per month for 30 years accruing $179,674 in interest.

A $250,000 mortgage at 3.5% costs $1,499.90 per month for 20 years accruing $97,076 in interest.

With only around a $300 monthly increase in cost it is possible to cut 10 years off your mortgage and save $81,698 in interest.

GOOD DEBT VERSUS BAD DEBT

For many people, debt is a necessary evil. While it is never ideal to borrow money, it is difficult to acquire items like a first home or college education without taking on debt. The key to deciding whether debt is "Good" or "Bad" is the asset that corresponds to your debt. Typically, good debt is tied to assets that are expected to appreciate in value (home purchase) or increase your earning potential (education).

EXAMPLES OF BAD DEBT:

– Credit card debt

– Payday loans

– Expensive auto debt (don't borrow $50,000 to buy a vehicle)

– Student loans for a masters degree that doesn't increase your earning potential

FINANCIAL PLAN CALCULATIONS

So, you've taken a financial inventory, but now what? The next aspect of creating a financial plan is running projections to model the income you can expect during your retirement years. This calculation can be done through a simple spreadsheet or through more advanced financial planning software. Regardless of which route you take, your goal is to find out if your money will last longer than you. To figure this out you'll need to project your financial inventory out for every year until your assumed date of death.

FORWARD PROJECTING CALCULATION

Beginning of year assets

+Income (adjusted for future inflation)   +Investment Returns

-Expenses (adjusted for future inflation)   -Taxes

=End of year assets

FORWARD PROJECTION EXAMPLE
$500,000 Starting Portfolio, $40,000 Annual Income Inflated at 2%, 7% investment Returns, $50,000 Annual Expenses Inflated at 3% and 20% Effective Tax Rate

Age	Beginning of Year Assets	Income	Investment Gains	Expenses	Taxes	End of Year Assets
70	$500,000.00	$40,000.00	$35,000.00	$50,000.00	$15,000.00	$510,000.00
71	$510,000.00	$40,800.00	$35,700.00	$51,500.00	$15,300.00	$519,700.00
72	$519,700.00	$41,616.00	$36,379.00	$53,045.00	$15,599.00	$529,051.00
73	$529,051.00	$42,448.32	$37,033.57	$54,636.35	$15,896.38	$538,000.16
74	$538,000.16	$43,297.29	$37,660.01	$56,275.44	$16,191.46	$546,490.56
75	$546,490.56	$44,163.23	$38,254.34	$57,963.70	$16,483.51	$554,460.91
76	$554,460.91	$45,046.50	$38,812.26	$59,702.61	$16,771.75	$561,845.31
77	$561,845.31	$45,947.43	$39,329.17	$61,493.69	$17,055.32	$568,572.89
78	$568,572.89	$46,866.38	$39,800.10	$63,338.50	$17,333.30	$574,567.57
79	$574,567.57	$47,803.70	$40,219.73	$65,238.66	$17,604.69	$579,747.66

Rate Risk

A key part to financial modeling of any type is using proper assumptions. A financial plan that uses inappropriate rate assumptions typically isn't worth the paper it is printed on. While it can be fun to be optimistic and assume your investments will return 15% annually, it is important to choose rate assumptions that have the best chance of projecting an accurate picture of your future.

INFLATION RATES

Inflation will dictate how much a dollar today is worth tomorrow. While inflation is unlikely to have much effect on your finances in the short-term, as you project 20 or more years out, inflation will have a huge effect on your expenses and financial plan because of its compounding effect. Just consider the price change of a Big Mac over the years.

Price Inflation of a Big Mac from 1994 to 2017[1]

Year	Price	Inflation
1994	$2.30	0.88%
1995	$2.32	0.87%
1996	$2.36	1.72%
1997	$2.42	2.54%
1998	$2.56	5.79%
1999	$2.43	-5.08%
2000	$2.51	3.29%
2001	$2.52	0.40%
2002	$2.49	-1.19%
2003	$2.71	8.84%
2004	$2.90	7.01%
2005	$3.06	5.52%
2006	$3.10	1.31%
2007	$3.22	3.87%
2008	$3.57	10.87%
2009	$3.57	0.00%
2010	$3.73	4.48%
2011	$3.80	1.88%
2012	$4.20	10.53%
2013	$4.33	3.10%
2014	$4.62	6.70%
2015	$4.79	3.68%
2016	$4.93	2.92%
2017	$5.06	2.64%
Average Inflation 3.44%		

[1]Data from *The Economist* – Sample data of cost of Big Mac in New York, Chicago, San Francisco & Atlanta.
Big Mac is copyright of McDonald's Corp.

Historical Inflation

U.S. inflation has ranged anywhere from as high as 13.5% in 1980 to as low as -0.4% in 2009. In your planning, it is safer to consider a higher rate of inflation. Since the government began tracking inflation in 1913, it has averaged 3.3% through 2014 according to the Consumer Price Index (CPI).

So what does a 2% inflation figure on $50,000 look like today versus a 3% or 5% number?

$50,000 compounded at 2% for 30 years equals $90,568

$50,000 compounded at 3% for 30 years equals $121,363

$50,000 compounded at 5% for 30 years equals $216,097

The difference between 2% and 5% in this scenario is a whopping $115,529! Obviously, inflation rates should not be underestimated in your financial and retirement planning.

RULE OF THUMB:
On average, prices double about every 20 years.

International Inflation

Inflation in the U.S. over the past century has been fairly tame thanks to U.S. dominance in global finance. While inflation will likely stay consistent in the U.S. over the coming decades, it's important to consider past examples in history where other countries have fallen from monetary grace. Just consider these past examples of hyperinflation that occurred in a single month of time.

Country	Year	Highest Single Monthly Inflation Rate
Russia	Jan. 1992	245%
Russia	Feb. 1924	212%
Germany	Oct. 1923	29,500%
Venezuela	Nov. 2016	221%
China	June 1945	302%

Source: The Hanke-Krus Hyperinflation Table - 2016

TAX RATES

In 1917, the top tax rate in the U.S. jumped from 15% up to 67% and eventually peaked at 94% in 1945. Luckily, today we enjoy a more friendly tax scheme; however, history has taught us that tax rates can change with the stroke of a pen. Odds are with an ever increasing U.S. national debt and steadily growing expenditures, it is probable that tax rates will increase in the future.

DEEP POCKETS — TAX RATES OVER THE PAST CENTURY

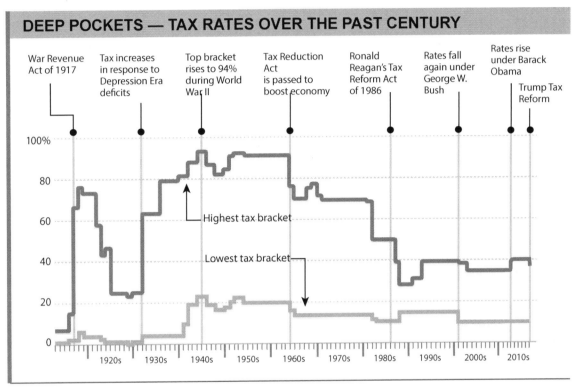

War Revenue Act of 1917

Tax increases in response to Depression Era deficits

Top bracket rises to 94% during World War II

Tax Reduction Act is passed to boost economy

Ronald Reagan's Tax Reform Act of 1986

Rates fall again under George W. Bush

Rates rise under Barack Obama

Trump Tax Reform

Highest tax bracket

Lowest tax bracket

Source: Internal Revenue Service

Nothing is certain except death and taxes, so you can count on still paying them during retirement. You will need to estimate your approximate tax rate you will be paying after your working years. Depending on your situation this rate may vary from the taxes you pay during employment. In order to estimate the taxes during retirement you need an understanding of the difference between marginal and effective tax rates.

Marginal Tax Rate

Your marginal tax rate is the rate of income tax paid on your last dollar of taxable income for the year. The US tax rate is progressive, meaning tax rates increase as your income rises.

2018 Federal Marginal Tax Brackets and Their Filing Status			
Tax Brackets	**Single**	**Married Filing Jointly**	**Head of Household**
10% Bracket	$0 – $9,525	$0 – $19,050	$0 – $13,600
12% Bracket	$9,526 – $38,700	$19,051 – $77,400	$13,601 – $51,800
22% Bracket	$38,701 – $82,500	$77,401 – $165,000	$51,801 – 82,500
24% Bracket	$82,501 – $157,500	$165,001 – $315,000	$82,501 – $157,500
32% Bracket	$157,501 – $200,000	$315,001 – $400,000	$157,501 – $200,000
35% Bracket	$200,001 - $500,000	$400,001 - $600,000	$200,001 - $500,000
37% Bracket	$500,001 and up	$600,001 and up	$500,001 and up

Source: Internal Revenue Service, 2018

Effective Tax Rate

The average amount of taxes you pay on your total taxable income is your effective tax rate. This rate will always be lower than your marginal tax rate.

Estimated 2018 Federal Effective Tax		
Taxable Income	**Single**	**Married Filing Jointly**
$25,000	11%	10%
$50,000	14%	11%
$100,000	18%	14%
$250,000	25%	19%
$1,000,000	34%	31%

Note: Percentages have been rounded.

Fun Fact: Not Paying Enough Taxes? The U.S. Treasury accepts voluntary payments to reduce the national debt. A $1,000,000 payment in 2017 would have funded the federal budget for approximately 7.6 seconds.

STATE AND LOCAL TAX RATES

In determining your total tax liability, your federal effective tax rate is only part of the picture. Individual states may have additional income and sales taxes. States like Florida with no income tax are popular for retirees for more than just the sunny weather.

How High Are Sales Taxes in Your State?
Combined State & Average Local Sales Tax Rates, 2016

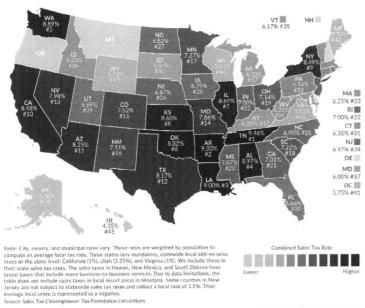

Note: City, county, and municipal rates vary. These rates are weighted by population to compute an average local tax rate. Three states levy mandatory, statewide local add-on sales taxes at the state level: California (1%), Utah (1.25%), and Virginia (1%). We include these in their state sales tax rates. The sales taxes in Hawaii, New Mexico, and South Dakota have broad bases that include many business-to-business services. Due to data limitations, the table does not include sales taxes in local resort areas in Montana. Some counties in New Jersey are not subject to statewide sales tax rates and collect a local rate of 3.5%. Their average local score is represented as a negative.
Source: Sales Tax Clearinghouse; Tax Foundation calculations.

Combined Sales Tax Rate — Lower / Higher

TAX FOUNDATION · @TaxFoundation

How High Are Income Tax Rates in Your State?
Top State Marginal Individual Income Tax Rates, 2016

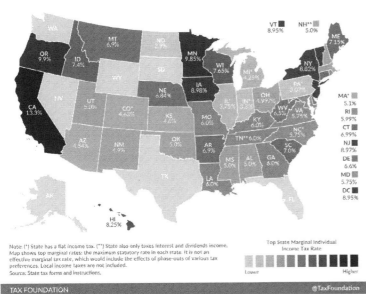

Note: (*) State has a flat income tax. (**) State also only taxes interest and dividends income. Map shows top marginal rates: the maximum statutory rate in each state. It is not an effective marginal tax rate, which would include the effects of phase-outs of various tax preferences. Local income taxes are not included.
Source: State tax forms and instructions.

Top State Marginal Individual Income Tax Rate — Lower / Higher

TAX FOUNDATION · @TaxFoundation

INVESTMENT RETURN RATES

The investment returns assumptions you use in your financial planning will be heavily dependent on your personal risk tolerance. As you might imagine, taking a greater amount of risk will typically reward you with higher returns over time. Consider these returns of the S&P 500 over the last 30 years which represent a broad basket of the 500 largest companies in the United States.

S&P 500 RETURNS OVER 30 YEARS 10.7% Annualized Returns					
Year	**Return**	**Year**	**Return**	**Year**	**Return**
1988	16.61%	1998	28.58%	2008	-37.00%
1989	31.69%	1999	21.04%	2009	26.46%
1990	-3.10%	2000	-9.10%	2010	15.06%
1991	30.47%	2001	-11.89%	2011	2.11%
1992	7.62%	2002	-22.10%	2012	16.00%
1993	10.08%	2003	28.68%	2013	32.39%
1994	1.32%	2004	10.88%	2014	13.69%
1995	37.58%	2005	4.91%	2015	1.40%
1996	22.96%	2006	15.79%	2016	11.96%
1997	33.36%	2007	5.49%	2017	21.83%
10 Year Average Return: 18.9%		**10 Year Average Return: 7.2%**		**10 Year Average Return: 10.4%**	

Source: S&P

Over the last 30 years the broad market has annualized returns of 10.7%. However, depending on the stretch of time you are looking at returns can vary significantly, and there has even been a 10 year subset period with a negative rate of return (2000-2009).

So, given that the markets have returned 10% over the last 30 years, is this a proper assumption to use in retirement planning? The answer is probably not. First of all, this return is for a 100% equity portfolio and also ignores any type of investment fees you may have incurred. After fees and diversification an aggressively invested portfolio would have been more likely to have seen returns of 7-9% over the past 30 years.

Perhaps you have the risk tolerance, time, and stomach to handle a 100% equity portfolio. Does it make sense to use this strategy during retirement? According to the next graph about withdrawal rates, probably not.

WITHDRAWAL RATE

"Withdrawal rate" is the pace at which you are drawing from your savings. For example, if you have $500,000 in savings, and you are withdrawing $20,000 annually then your withdrawal rate is 4%.

ANNUAL WITHDRAWALS / SAVINGS = WITHDRAWAL RATE

Choosing a successful withdrawal rate is one of the more complicated processes in retirement planning. It is a function of inflation, longevity, and investment returns. Choose a rate too high and you risk going broke, too low and you may not enjoy retirement. Find a balance.

RULE OF THUMB:

A 4% withdrawal rate has historically been successful based on long-term stock market returns and inflation figures in the United States.

Consider the following hypothetical return sequences, each with an average annual return of 8% and a withdrawal rate of 4% (starting with $500,000 in total assets).

SEQUENCE OF RETURNS								
$500,000 Starting Portfolio with $20,000 End-of-Year Distribution								
Steady Growth			**Down Late**			**Down Early**		
Year	ROR	Year-end Total	Year	ROR	Year-end Total	Year	ROR	Year-end Total
1	8%	$520,000	1	40%	$680,000	1	-30%	$330,000
2	8%	$541,600	2	40%	$932,000	2	-10%	$277,000
3	8%	$564,928	3	20%	$1,098,400	3	-10%	$229,300
4	8%	$590,122	4	10%	$1,188,240	4	0%	$209,300
5	8%	$617,332	5	10%	$1,287,064	5	10%	$210,230
6	8%	$646,719	6	10%	$1,395,770	6	10%	$211,253
7	8%	$678,456	7	0%	$1,375,770	7	10%	$212,378
8	8%	$712,733	8	-10%	$1,218,193	8	20%	$234,854
9	8%	$749,751	9	-10%	$1,076,374	9	40%	$308,796
10	8%	$789,731	10	-30%	$733,462	10	40%	$412,314
Average Return: 8% **Ending Assets: $789,731**			**Average Return: 8%** **Ending Assets: $733,462**			**Average Return: 8%** **Ending Assets: $412,314**		

The lesson learned is that all investment returns are not created equal! Large investment losses are more damaging in retirement when you are taking withdrawals in addition to losing value.

DOLLAR COST AVERAGING

In contrast to the previous withdrawal rate example, during the accumulation phase of retirement planning volatility can be your friend. Down years can turn out to be much less painful thanks to the benefits of dollar cost averaging. If an investor is saving and investing on a consistent basis, then down years and lower prices allow for purchasing more stock, so that when the markets recover there is actually that much more in the pot to increase in value.

SEQUENCE OF RETURNS $500,000 Starting Portfolio with $20,000 End-of-Year Addition								
Steady Growth			Down Late			Down Early		
Year	ROR	Year-end Total	Year	ROR	Year-end Total	Year	ROR	Year-end Total
1	8%	$560,000	1	40%	$720,000	1	-30%	$370,000
2	8%	$624,800	2	40%	$1,028,000	2	-10%	$353,000
3	8%	$694,784	3	20%	$1,253,600	3	-10%	$337,700
4	8%	$770,367	4	10%	$1,398,960	4	0%	$357,700
5	8%	$851,996	5	10%	$1,558,856	5	10%	$413,470
6	8%	$940,156	6	10%	$1,734,742	6	10%	$474,817
7	8%	$1,035,368	7	0%	$1,754,742	7	10%	$542,299
8	8%	$1,138,198	8	-10%	$1,599,267	8	20%	$670,758
9	8%	$1,249,253	9	-10%	$1,459,341	9	40%	$959,062
10	8%	$1,369,194	10	-30%	$1,041,538	10	40%	$1,362,687
Average Return: 8% Ending Assets: $1,369,194			Average Return: 8% Ending Assets: $1,041,538			Average Return: 8% Ending Assets: $1,362,687		

As you can see, the mathematics of volatile returns are quite different depending on your stage in life. So, in retirement strongly consider opportunities to lower investment volatility and target consistent returns.

LONGEVITY AND HEALTH CARE EXPENSES

When Social Security was created in 1935, very few people enjoyed retirements that lasted multiple decades. In fact, in 1940 only 56.5% of adults lived to become 65 or older.[2] However, today as health care and medicine continue to advance, it is possible that many people nearing retirement will enjoy retirements of 40 years or more.

Long life is a good problem (for most), but it does bring about planning concerns. Be careful not to underestimate your life span in your retirement planning. Life expectancies are just averages, and as you can imagine, very few people die on the exact day of their life expectancy (currently 78 years and 3 months).[3]

If you are a healthy 65-year-old, you have a 25% chance of living to the age of 92 for a man and age 94 for a woman.[4] This means your money may need to last more than 30 years.

With longer life also comes increased health care expenses. Over the last several decades, inflation in health care has significantly outpaced overall inflation and has been on average over 6% for the past decade. Should this pattern continue, health expenses will unfortunately be a larger and larger percentage of everyone's expenses.

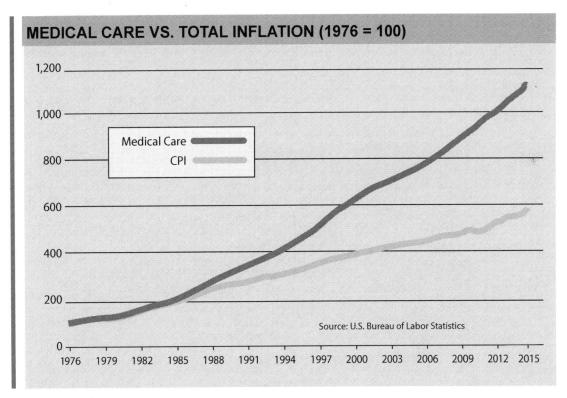

MEDICAL CARE VS. TOTAL INFLATION (1976 = 100)

Source: U.S. Bureau of Labor Statistics

Medicare begins once you reach age 65, so for anyone planning to retire prior to eligibility, it is crucial to bridge any lapses in health insurance. Going without health insurance is a quick way to deplete a lifetime of savings.

[2]Social Security Administration
[3]The World Bank Annual Report - 2012
[4]Society of Actuaries Data

LONGEVITY FUN FACTS

– People born to mothers under age 25 have a greater chance of living to 100.

– People who live in rural or low-income areas tend to have shorter lives.

– The heaviest 15% of the population have significantly lowered chances of living to old age.

– Wealthier, highly educated, and married populations tend to live longer.

– Those born from September through November tend to live to 100 more often than others.

LONG TERM CARE EXPENSES

The cost of long-term care is something that should not be ignored in retirement planning. Approximately two thirds of those who reach age 65 will utilize long-term care services in their lifetime. Medicare is not designed to cover the bulk of an extended stay in a long-term care facility. Additionally, Medicaid will only cover these expenses once you have spent the majority of your assets. If you have a surviving spouse, or desire to leave a legacy, then Medicaid is not an ideal option for retirement planning.

Long-term care insurance has been designed to alleviate many of the risks associated with health care expenses in retirement. It is discussed further in the Risk Management Chapter.

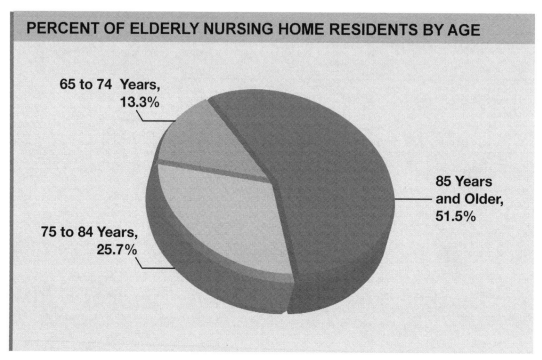

PERCENT OF ELDERLY NURSING HOME RESIDENTS BY AGE

65 to 74 Years, 13.3%

85 Years and Older, 51.5%

75 to 84 Years, 25.7%

Source: 2005 statistical abstract of the United States

DO I NEED A PROFESSIONAL?

During the financial planning process, you might find tasks in which you are better off relying on professional help instead of going it on your own (filing taxes, investing, estate planning, etc.). When deciding whether you need professional help or not, you must first figure out the complexity of your current needs in addition to knowing your own skill set. Also, many tasks such as taxes and investment management involve staying up-to-date on complex issues, which can take a significant amount of time and energy.

Designation Alphabet Soup

According to www.wiseradvisor.com, there are over 100 designations in the financial industry. This surplus of designations makes it that much more difficult for the average consumer to find qualified professional help. Any good designation must be comprehensive in nature, with significant experience and educational requirements.

Designation	Specialty	College Level Classes	Comp. Test	Experience Required	College Degree Required
Comprehensive					
CFA—Chartered Financial Analyst	Investments	2 Years	Yes	3 Years	Bachelor
CFP—Certified Financial Planner	Comprehensive Planning	1 Year	Yes	3 Years	Bachelor
CLU—Chartered Life Underwriter	Insurance	1 Year	No	3 Years	Bachelor
CPA—Certified Public Accountant	Taxes & Accounting	1 Year	Yes	1 Year	Bachelor
JD—Juris Doctorate	Estate Planning	3 Years	Yes	1 Year	Masters
Less Comprehensive					
CRPC—Certified Retirement Planning Counselor	Retirement Planning	2 Weeks	No	None	None
CIMA—Certified Investment Management Analyst	Investments	2 Weeks	No	3 Years	None
FA—Financial Advisor	None	None	None	None	None

CHAPTER 2:

TAXES

PREPARING FOR RETIREMENT

A Comprehensive Guide to Financial Planning

TAXES

Tax planning is an important part of the financial and retirement planning process. In fact, it's one of the few parts of the process that is absolutely required to be done each and every year (typically around the April 15 filing deadline). A better understanding of the tax code can help you effectively (and legally) lower your tax bill, thus maximizing your retirement savings.

Our current tax structure is progressive in nature where the highest income earners bear the largest tax burden. In 2014, the bottom 50% of earners paid 2.7% of all income taxes while the top 10% accounted for 70.9%.

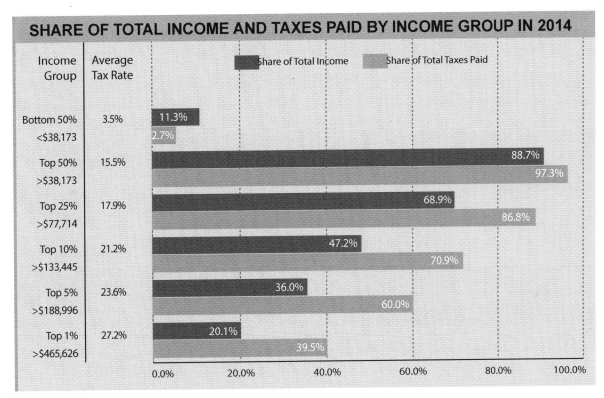

SHARE OF TOTAL INCOME AND TAXES PAID BY INCOME GROUP IN 2014

Income Group	Average Tax Rate	Share of Total Income	Share of Total Taxes Paid
Bottom 50% <$38,173	3.5%	11.3%	2.7%
Top 50% >$38,173	15.5%	88.7%	97.3%
Top 25% >$77,714	17.9%	68.9%	86.8%
Top 10% >$133,445	21.2%	47.2%	70.9%
Top 5% >$188,996	23.6%	36.0%	60.0%
Top 1% >$465,626	27.2%	20.1%	39.5%

Source: Federal Income Tax Data, 2014

COMPONENTS OF TAXABLE INCOME

Generally, the following items are counted toward your gross income:

- Wages, salaries, bonuses, tips
- Business income (loss)
- Taxable interest
- Capital gains (losses)
- Dividends
- Alimony (Prior to 2019)
- Taxable Social Security (Up to 85%)
- IRA distributions
- Pensions and annuities
- Rental real estate profits
- Punitive damages awarded from a lawsuit or settlement
- Unemployment income
- Farm income

Exclusions from Gross Income

The following items are typically excluded from gross income:

- Municipal bond income
- Deferrals to an employer-sponsored retirement plan
- Life insurance proceeds
- Adoption expense reimbursements for qualifying expenses
- Child support payments
- Gifts, bequests and inheritances
- Workers' compensation benefits (some exceptions may apply; see Publication 525, Taxable and Nontaxable Income)
- Flexible spending accounts
- Scholarships
- Meals and lodging for the convenience of your employer
- Compensatory damages from lawsuit or settlement
- Welfare benefits
- Cash rebates from a dealer or manufacturer

Adjusted Gross Income (AGI)

Your AGI is the amount of income (before deductions) on which you owe taxes.

Total gross income minus adjustments to income = AGI

Potential Adjustments to Gross Income

- Deductible retirement plan contributions
- Health Savings Account contributions
- Educator expenses
- Student loan interest

- Self-employed health or long term care insurance
- 1/2 self-employment taxes
- Alimony paid (For divorces that become finalized in 2019 or later, alimony payments will no longer be deductible to the payor, nor includable as income to the payee.

Modified Adjusted Gross Income (MAGI)

MAGI is primarily used to determine eligibility for IRA deductions.

AGI + these commonly added back items (not all are shown):

- Deductions for traditional IRA contributions that are deductible
- Municipal bond interest
- Deductions claimed for student loan interest or qualified tuition expenses

Personal Exemption (Currently Repealed)

Taxpayers used to be allowed to claim a tax benefit for themselves and any dependent that they provided the majority of support for. This provision was repealed as part of the 2017 Tax Cuts and Jobs Act. A larger standard deduction replaced this exemption.

Standard Deduction

Taxpayers are able to deduct against AGI the greater of the standard deduction or their itemized deductions. The standard deduction increased in 2018:

Single	Head of Household	Married Filing Jointly	Married Filing Separately	Qualifying Widow/Widower
$12,000	$18,000	$24,000	$12,000	$24,000

Itemized Deductions (Changed in 2018)

Itemized deductions may include the following:

– Medical expenses (amount exceeding 7.5% of AGI in 2018 and 10% afterwards)

– State and local income, property or sales tax (SALT) capped at $10,000

– Mortgage interest (limits apply)

– Margin interest

– Job-related education and professional development (non-reimbursed)

– Gambling losses (to the extent they offset gambling income)

– Fair market value contributions to charities and churches

Deductions Repealed in 2018

– Mortgage interest from home equity loans

– Personal losses because of theft or casualty (except in federally declared disasters)

– Job-related expenses that were not reimbursed by employer

– Tax preparation fees and certain investment fees (miscellaneous fees)

Charitable Donations

The 2017 tax reform bill increases the maximum taxpayers can donate to charities, raising the limit to 60% of adjusted gross income from 50%.

When giving charitable donations, it is generally more effective to donate highly appreciated assets instead of cash (stocks, collectibles, etc.). By doing so, the donor receives a deduction for the entire fair market value of the donation and escapes paying capital gains taxes on the assets. If securities are sold and after-tax proceeds donated, the donor and charity will receive a lesser benefit.

Pass-Through Service Based Income

One of the most significant pieces of the 2017 Tax Cuts and Jobs Act was a change in the taxation of small business pass-through income. For personal service businesses, including realtors, attorneys, health care and financial services there is up to a 20% deduction of the qualified business income (QBI) of each individual.

This deduction is only available for joint filers with incomes up to $315,000 and $157,500 for single taxpayers.

Alternative Minimum Tax (AMT)

As of 1969 each year a taxpayer must pay the greater of their normal tax bill or their Alternative Minimum Tax amount. As income rises certain tax exemptions may be lost thus causing a taxpayer to pay the potentially higher AMT calculation.

As originally drafted the AMT affected very few taxpayers, however, after the initial threshold was not adjusted for inflation in decades this tax mechanism affected a far greater percentage of people. The 2017 Tax Cuts and Jobs act reformed AMT indexing exemption thresholds for inflation going forward:

Filing Status	AMT Exemption	AMT Phase-out Level
2018 AMT Thresholds and Exemptions by Filing Status		
Single	$70,300	$500,000
Joint	$109,400	$1,000,000
2017 AMT Thresholds and Exemptions by Filing Status		
Single	$54,300	$120,700
Joint	$84,500	$160,900

TAX CLASSIFICATIONS

It's nice to own stocks, bonds, and other investments. Nice, that is, until it's time to fill out your federal income tax return. At that point, you may be left scratching your head. Just how do you report your investments, and how are they taxed?

Most investment income falls into the three following categories:

Ordinary Income	Capital Gains	Dividends

Ordinary Income

All the following investments are subject to ordinary income tax rates:

- Interest (money market, CD, savings, bond)

- Non-qualified dividends

- Distributions from a qualified retirement account (401(k), 403(b), IRA)

- Income from a partnership

DID YOU KNOW?

In 2010, there were 1.2 million tax preparers in the US, more than the number of police and firefighters combined.

Annuity Taxation

All investment gains from annuities are classified as ordinary income. However, these gains are only realized once liquidated and removed from the shelter of the annuity. Should an annuity owner pass away, their heirs will still owe ordinary income taxes on gains within the annuity, and there will be no step-up in cost basis.

CAPITAL GAINS TAXES

Capital Gains

Almost everything an individual owns could be considered a capital asset. Stocks, rental houses, boats, or other similar assets sold at an appreciated value may be subject to capital gains taxes.

Capital gains and losses are categorized as either short-term or long-term based on whether an asset was held 12 months or less. Short-term capital gains are taxed at ordinary income tax rates while long-term capital gains are taxed more favorably:

Long-Term Capital Gains Rate	Single Taxpayer	Married Filing Jointly	Head of Household	Married Filing Separately
0%	Up to $38,600	Up to $77,200	Up to $51,700	Up to $38,600
15%	$38,600-$425,800	$77,200-$479,000	$51,700-$452,400	$38,600-$239,500
20%	Over $425,800	Over $479,000	Over $452,400	Over $239,500

Note: Long-term capital gains on collectibles are taxed at 28%.

Strategy: After retirement you may have a time period of very low income before turning on Social Security or pension benefits. This can potentially be a great time to liquidate appreciated assets and pay a 0% capital gains rate.

Capital Losses

When investing, any investor could potentially lose money. Should you incur more capital losses in a given year than capital gains, you can deduct up to $3,000 in losses for that year (for married filing jointly taxpayers). Excess losses are carried forward to future years.

Example: An investor sold a rental property for a $25,000 loss in 2008. Additionally, he lost $15,000 in the stock market, making a $40,000 total capital loss for the year. For 2008, he may deduct $3,000 from his taxable income and carry forward the remaining $37,000 to future years. In 2009, the investor made $50,000 in the stock market. $37,000 of these gains will be offset, leaving a taxable gain of only $13,000 for 2009.

Wash-Sale Rule

If selling assets to realize losses, be careful if you intend on repurchasing them within a short time frame. Investors must wait 30 days after a realized loss to repurchase an asset to avoid the loss on the initial sale from being disallowed.

DIVIDEND TAX

A dividend is a sum of money paid regularly (typically quarterly) by a company to its shareholders out of its profits. Dividends will vary from company to company and many companies pay none at all. Many investors choose to reinvest dividends where the proceeds buy more of the stock or mutual fund that distributed the dividend. Even if you reinvest dividends, you will still be liable for any tax due on the distribution. Currently, dividends are classified as either qualified or non-qualified.

QUALIFIED DIVIDENDS

- Subject to same tax treatment as long-term capital gains

- Must be paid by an American company or qualifying foreign company

- Subject to a dividend holding period (total of 60 days between the window of 60 days before and after the ex-dividend date)

NON-QUALIFIED DIVIDENDS

- Subject to ordinary income tax rates

- Dividends from REITs and preferred stocks are typically non-qualified

Affordable Care Act "Unearned" Income Medicare Tax

In 2013 a new tax came into effect for households with taxable income over $250,000 for those married filing jointly or $200,000 for single filing tax payers. The provision applies a 3.8% surcharge tax on "unearned" investment income such as interest, dividends, and capital gains.

Example: A household with $300,000 in gross income has $50,000 in long-term capital gains. The $50,000 would be taxed at a total rate of 18.8% ($9,400) which would be the normal 15% long-term capital gains rate plus the 3.8% surcharge.

MUTUAL FUND TAXES

Mutual funds are required to distribute dividends and capital gains at least once a year.

RULE OF THUMB

Mutual funds typically distribute capital gains in the last two months of the year.

Mutual fund capital gains distributions go to all current owners of the fund regardless of whether their mutual fund shares have appreciated in value. Capital gains distributions are based on the underlying sales within the fund, which are typically not visible to the individual investor. For this reason, investors must be careful when purchasing mutual funds toward year-end.

EXAMPLE:

– Investor purchases $25,000 of FUNDX, 1,000 shares at $25/share on December 20th.

– On December 21st, FUNDX distributes a long-term capital gain of $2/share that is reinvested.

– The investor still has $25,000 of FUNDX, but now has 1086.956 shares at $23/share.

– Unfortunately, the investor now owes long-term capital gains tax on $2,000 in gains even though he has not realized any profit from his fund ownership.

Qualified Accounts

A qualified account is an investment that is not subject to taxation until a distribution is taken. Thus, investment gains and income within a qualified account are not currently taxable or included in a taxpayer's gross income. Examples of qualified investment vehicles include: Traditional IRA, 401(k) plan, 403(b) plan, Simple IRA, SEP-IRA, 457 Plan.

Non-qualified investment vehicles include everything else—savings accounts, brokerage accounts, real estate, etc.

QUALIFIED ACCOUNT QUALITIES

– Grows tax deferred	– No deductions for losses
– Contributions = typically pre-tax/deductible	– 10% penalty for distributions prior to 55 or 59½
– No taxes as gains are realized	– Required minimum distributions (RMD) at 70½
– Withdrawals taxed at ordinary income rates	– Income and contribution limits may apply

CHAPTER 3:

REAL ESTATE

PREPARING FOR RETIREMENT

A Comprehensive Guide to Financial Planning

Real estate typically represents a significant portion of a household's net worth in the United States. In fact, at a combined $20.7 trillion, primary residences accounted for 30% of all assets held by households in 2010 (www.nahb.org). Thus, when reviewing one's overall financial picture, it would be prudent to examine your real estate holdings. Outside of just providing us shelter, real estate can also be a valuable investment vehicle and tool for passing wealth onto future generations.

When dealing with real estate, it is extremely important to know that housing markets are very localized. Different markets can have large discrepancies in values for seemingly identical homes. So, it is important utilize a variety of resources before entering into a real estate transaction.

As of 2017, the median housing price in the United States was $315,200, up 3.7% from a year earlier. However, the average value of a house varies greatly from state to state. In 2017 the average listing price of a home in Hawaii was nearly $1 million versus several states in the Midwest with values under $200,000.

Highest Average Listing Price		Lowest Average Listing Price	
Hawaii	$905,687	Alabama	$212,733
District of Columbia	$773,286	Missouri	$204,506
California	$697,539	Oklahoma	$201,091
Massachusetts	$602,210	Mississippi	$195,390
New York	$565,227	Arkansas	$191,446
Colorado	$538,477	Indiana	$190,843
Utah	440,946	Ohio	$190,371
Connecticut	$435,585	Kansas	$187,649
Oregon	$416,718	Iowa	$185,087
Florida	$406,803	West Virginia	$174,865

Source: Trulia.com, Aug. 2017 Average Listing Values by State

MORTGAGES

As of December 2017, property owners had a total of $14.7 trillion in mortgage debt outstanding. While that is an enormous amount, it is still 25% less than where the Federal Government ended the year at $20 trillion in debt (www.federalreserve.gov). Due to the large purchase price of real estate it is not unusual for individuals or businesses to finance property acquisitions via a mortgage.

Mortgage Terms

When selecting a mortgage the most important factor to consider is going to be the term of the payments. If you can afford it, typically the shorter the mortgage period you select the better. The reason for this is twofold. First, a shorter mortgage period will usually be accompanied with a lower interest rate. Second, and more importantly, a shorter term mortgage will experience less compounding of interest and a faster accumulation of equity. Below contrast the difference between the standard 15, 20, and 30 year fixed rate mortgages:

MORTGAGE INTEREST COMPARISON			
	15 Year Mortgage	20 Year Mortgage	30 Year Mortgage
Mortgage Amount	$300,000	$300,000	$300,000
Interest Rate	3.50%	3.75%	4.00%
Monthly Payment	$2,145	$1,779	$1,432
Total Payments	$386,100	$426,960	$515,520
Total Interest	$86,100	$126,960	$215,520

In the above example of a $300,000 mortgage, a home owner would have realized $88,560 in interest savings by selecting the 20 year instead of a 30 year term mortgage. These savings and a payment term that is 10 years shorter can be realized by an extra $347 per month cash outflow.

Fixed Rate Versus ARMs

Adjustable rate mortgages (ARMs) differ from fixed rate mortgages in that they have an interest rate that may fluctuate on set intervals. According to www.bankrate.com, 1 in 5 mortgage applicants select an adjustable rate mortgage.

The most popular ARM products typically have rates that will vary on 2, 5, and 7 year terms. What this means is that the interest rate will fluctuate every 2, 5, or 7 years depending on your product selection. Most lenders currently index ARM products to interest rates tied to either U.S. treasury bonds or LIBOR (London Interbank Offered Rates). So, if interest rates have gone up on the anniversary of your ARM, then your rate and payment will ratchet up as well. Conversely, if interest rates have fallen then your payment and interest cost may decrease. When selecting an ARM, it is extremely important to consider how long you plan on living in a home, in addition to the impact a change in interest rates may have on your personal finances. While you may save close to 1% in the early years, consider the impact should your rate jump 2% or more in the future.

LENGTH OF HOME OWNERSHIP

When considering your financing needs, it is important to estimate the length of time you plan on being in a home. Your ideal mortgage options will vary greatly depending on if you plan on living in a home for five years or five decades. According to the NAHB, the average amount of time home buyers stay in a home is 13.3 years. So, if you are a first time home buyer planning on staying in a home 10 years or less, it may be ideal to choose a 7 year Adjustable Rate Mortgage because you'll have minimum financial risk from future rate hikes.

ESTIMATED YEARS UNTIL HALF OF SINGLE-FAMILY BUYERS MOVE OUT

RULE OF THUMB:

If you are uncertain whether you will live in a home 5 years or longer you are most likely better off renting a home or apartment instead. After buy and sell transaction costs it is unlikely you will come out ahead. Also, home ownership may pose financial difficulties if your career requires regular relocating.

Mortgages in Retirement Planning

Another important aspect of mortgage planning is considering how the term of your mortgage aligns with your retirement goals. A fully paid off mortgage lowers the amount of income you'll need to retire, thus lowering the amount of capital you'll need to accumulate before retirement. If you are considering an early retirement, investing in a shorter term mortgage that matches your expected retirement target date can simplify your budgeting and cash flow management. However, if you plan on working until age 70 or later, then your finances can most likely support a longer term mortgage.

Home Equity Line of Credit (HELOC)

A home equity line of credit is a loan one can get that is collateralized by the equity in your home. These types of loans typically have a variable interest rate, but due to their convenience and low fees, can be a valuable tool in financial planning, especially as a source of liquidity for emergencies or large purchases.

MORTGAGE QUALIFICATION

If you are looking to purchase a home, but you have no clue what mortgage amount you currently qualify for, there are some simple ratios your lender will use to pre-qualify you.

Debt to Income Ratios

The primary factor in determining the maximum amount of housing debt a lender will provide is the debt to income ratio. For a conventional loan these ratios are 28% and 36%.

The lower 28% figure is the ratio of your mortgage payment compared to your total income.

Total Income ($100,000) X 28% = $28,000 per year or $2,333/month for house payments.

The higher 36% ratio is for the second qualifying factor, and that is the ratio of your total debt in relation to your total income.

Total Income ($100,000) X 36% = $36,000 per year or $3,000/month for all debt payments.

So, if you have no current debt on your balance sheet, the only calculation you will need to worry about is the 28% mortgage debt to income ratio. However, if you have student loans, vehicle debt, or revolving credit card balances you will need to add up all your monthly payments.

Certain individuals may have further wiggle room on these ratios in the mortgage process. There are programs offered by the government that may provide greater flexibility to home buyers. Loans provided by the Federal Housing Association (FHA) and the Veteran's Administration (VA) have a more liberal 41% ratio allowed for total debt to total income. However, consumers will potentially pay more for these products as FHA-backed loans carried a rate that is on average 0.375% higher than a similar conventional loan at the end of 2014 (www.hsh.com).

Down Payments and Private Mortgage Insurance

Conventional mortgages currently require at least a 5% down payment. So, if the purchase price of a house was $500,000, at least a $25,000 down payment would be needed to acquire a conventional loan.

The size of your down payment will affect whether your lender will require Private Mortgage Insurance (PMI). If you purchase a property with less than a 20% down payment then your lender will require PMI until you reach 20% equity in your property. PMI costs vary, but typically they run 0.5% to 1% annually of the property's purchase price. So, PMI costs on a $500,000 property would be $2,500-$5,000 each year. While it wasn't always the case, PMI costs are now available as an itemized deduction for some home owners, in addition to their mortgage interest expense.

VACATION PROPERTY

So far we have concentrated only on real estate classified as a "primary residence". Typically this is the property you spend the majority of your time in and use for tax planning purposes. However, many people have second homes (or third or fourth) that are regularly utilized. Many people dream of having a vacation property and it is a core retirement goal. So what are the advantages and disadvantages of owning a vacation home versus renting?

Advantages	Disadvantages
Schedule Flexibility	Mortgage or Capital Expenses
Home Customization	Insurance Expense
Potential Rental Income	Repair Expense
Potential Price Appreciation	Lack flexibility in changing properties
	HOA Dues
	Property Taxes

The most important financial aspect of considering a vacation property is to determine your personal utilization rate. Your personal utilization rate is the percentage of the year you plan on actively using your vacation property. As you might imagine, the higher the utilization rate the better the value there is to owning your own vacation home.

However, just because you don't plan on living for months on end in your vacation property doesn't mean it cannot make financial sense. If you only plan on utilizing your property for a fraction of the year it is important to consider leasing your property for the remaining portion of the year. Most vacation locales have property management companies that can facilitate the rental process and cleaning of your property so that the owner doesn't have to shoulder the burden from afar. If you can't find a property manager, then there are also vacation property websites like www.vrbo.com and www.homeaway.com that can take care of the marketing of your property. After all, it is difficult to find a renter if no one knows about your house. According to Jon Gray of HomeAway, "Nearly half of the people who finance their vacation homes are able to cover 75 percent or more of their mortgage by renting it out to travelers".

Vacation Home Taxability

Your personal utilization rate of your vacation home will also have important tax repercussions. If you are the primary user of your property, then you are able to rent the unit for up to 14 days per year and the income from the rental is federal income tax free.

Second Home as Full-Time Rental

You may have a vacation home that you only utilize a few days a year and then rent out beyond those days. If you personally use a property for 14 or fewer days, or 10% of the time it is rented, then you can potentially convert your property to an investment property for tax purposes.

INVESTMENT PROPERTY

Investment properties differ from your personal residence in that the primary goal of such a property is to make a profit over time. Many investors prefer investments in real estate versus the stock and bond market. A well-constructed real estate portfolio can deliver consistent and predictable cash flows, and in conjunction with prudent leverage via mortgages it can provide significant long term investment returns. However, real estate takes significantly more effort to properly manage than a stock or bond portfolio, so a decision to be a landlord isn't for everyone.

Investment Property Mortgages

When looking to finance an investment property with debt there are some important differences compared to a primary residence. The first difference is the down payment requirement. Investment properties typically require at least a 20-30% down payment on the purchase price versus the 5% requirement on a personal residence. In addition to the added down payment cost, borrowers can also expect to pay a 1-3% higher interest rate than they would see for their primary residence. For this reason, it isn't unusual for an individual to instead borrow money against their primary residence and then use that cash to invest in other properties.

Depreciation

Investment properties also vary from your personal residence in that investors are allowed to claim depreciation annually. When an asset is depreciated for tax purposes a certain percentage of the value of the asset is written off each year against income generated by the asset. For example, the IRS deems a useful life of 27.5 years for the depreciation schedule of residential real estate. So, if you purchase a property for $150,000, of which the tax assessment is $100,000 home value and $50,000 land value (land cannot be depreciated), the IRS would allow you to depreciate the $100,000 home value over 27.5 years which would equate into a $3636 annual deduction.

$$\$100,000 / 27.5 \text{ years} = \$3,636.36$$

As you can imagine depreciation can greatly increase the tax efficiency of owning and investing in real estate. However, taking depreciation isn't a completely free lunch. When you depreciate a property, it lowers your cost basis in the property, and should you sell the property at a gain then that depreciation will be "recaptured" and taxed at ordinary income tax rates instead of the more beneficial long term capital gains rate.

RULE OF THUMB:

Be careful when investing in real estate or any other asset via leverage. If a portfolio only has 20% equity, then a 20% decrease in property value will wipe out the entire net worth of the portfolio.

REAL ESTATE CAPITAL GAINS TAXATION

The Tax Payer Relief Act of 1997 allowed single taxpayers an exclusion of $250,000 ($500,000 for married filing jointly) on capital gains incurred on the sale of a primary residence. Prior to this law there was a once in a lifetime exclusion of $125,000 for individuals over 55 years old.

For this exclusion to apply, the property being sold must be the taxpayer's primary residence for at least two of the last five years. It is not necessary that the two years be consecutive. As a result of this rule, the exclusion can only be claimed once every two years. This income exclusion also applies to the 3.8% Affordable Care Act investment income surcharge.

Second Home Exclusions

The housing law enacted on July 30, 2008, placed an additional restriction on the exclusion of gain from the sale of a principal residence. If there is a period of "non-qualified use" after 2008, the portion of a taxpayer's gain allocated to that period won't qualify for the exclusion. The provision primarily affects taxpayers who own vacation homes or rental properties but convert them to a principal residence for a period of at least two years prior to sale.

Example: You've owned a vacation home for many years and would like to sell it. You expect to have a gain of $350,000, and the entire gain would be taxable because you haven't used the property as your principal residence. Rather than sell it now, you and your spouse make this home your principal residence for a period of two years, after which you sell it for a gain of $400,000. The home now qualifies as a principal residence.

Previously, this arrangement would make it possible to exclude all the gain because you're allowed an exclusion of up to $500,000 on a joint return. (A recapture rule applies to depreciation deductions, but in this example you didn't claim any depreciation.) Under the new law, part of your gain would be taxable but only to the extent you have non-qualified use of the property after 2008.

A tax or legal advisor should be consulted if trying to use the personal residence exclusion on an investment property.

1031 Property Exchanges

When exchanging "business" property, one may be able to take advantage of what is termed a "like-kind exchange," in which no gain or loss will be realized under the Internal Revenue section 1031. When executing a "like-kind exchange," one must be purchasing an asset that is the same in nature and character, and the total replacement asset must be equal to or greater than the total net sales price of the property being sold.

Rules and timing regarding a 1031 exchange are complicated, and you should always consult with a tax or legal advisor if considering a 1031 exchange.

CHAPTER 4:

INVESTMENTS

PREPARING FOR RETIREMENT

A COMPREHENSIVE GUIDE TO FINANCIAL PLANNING

INVESTMENTS

The past decade has seen a huge shift away from guaranteed pension plans for retirement income toward self-directed retirement plans. Because of this shift, the need for sound investment management has never been greater.

THIS CHAPTER WILL COVER THE FOLLOWING:

– Loaning versus owning

– Cash reserves

– Fixed income and bonds

– Stocks

– Mutual funds

– Exchange-traded funds

– Alternative investments

Loaning Versus Owning

Fundamentally, there are two basic ways to invest:

– Loaning your money

– Purchasing and owning assets

LOANING

Many of the most common forms of investments are actually loans. Whether you have a savings account at the bank, a CD, or a bond, you are actually a creditor to the organization that has your funds.

For your loan, the borrower guarantees to:

• repay the principal investment at par value

• pay interest in return for the use of the money

Remember, the guarantees on your investment are only as good as the issuer. Many loan based investments may also have secondary guarantees should the primary borrower become insolvent.

OWNING

Another type of investment is the actual purchase and ownership stake in a company or asset. Common examples are stocks, real estate, gold or a small business. Owners receive the following:

• The potential for the investment to appreciate in value

• No guarantees on investment principal

• Potential for distributions of profits or dividends

• Potential voting interest to affect company decisions

RULE OF THUMB:

The Rule of 72 is a simple method used to estimate the time it will take for an investment to double in value. 72 ÷ rate of return = # of years to double your money.

CASH RESERVES

Type of Account	Description
Cash Account	Cash accounts are one example of a loan based investment. There are many types of cash based accounts, and many are considered "cash equivalents."
Savings Account	Savings accounts typically have low minimum balances, excellent liquidity and low rates of interest. They are usually FDIC insured.
Certificate of Deposit (CD)	CDs require an investment for a specified period of time, and CDs shorter than 6 months are typically considered a cash equivalent. Typically, CDs pay a higher interest rate than savings accounts but may incur penalties if liquidated before maturity. They are usually FDIC insured.
Money Market Accounts	Money market accounts operate similarly to savings accounts and may also have check writing functions. They typically have a variable interest rate and are usually FDIC insured.
Money Market Mutual Funds	This variety of money market account is typically NOT FDIC insured. It is functionally similar to a regular money market account, but the borrower reinvests funds in short-term government and corporate debt. Some may invest in short-term municipal bonds, thus providing tax-free interest payments.

Liquidity

Liquidity is best described as how efficiently an asset can be converted to cash (can you get what it's worth). A lack of accessible cash in retirement can be a cause for lowered investment returns and possible penalties (annuity or CD surrender penalties, for example).

RULE OF THUMB:

Keep 6 to 12 months of expenses "liquid" in retirement. The more risk averse you are, the more liquid assets you should keep on hand. Remember, just because you're retired doesn't mean that emergencies won't happen. Cars will still break down; roofs will still leak; and, unfortunately, family emergencies will still occur.

FDIC INSURANCE

FDIC insurance is a crucial part of cash account investments. The Federal Deposit Insurance Corporation (FDIC) was set up in 1933 as a direct result of the bank failures of the Great Depression. The system is funded by premiums collected from participating institutions. Credit Unions have equivalent insurance that is managed by the National Credit Union Administration.

Each depositor insured to at least $250,000
Backed by the full faith and credit of the United States government

Federal Deposit Insurance Corporation-www.fdic.gov

If you have a cash investment at a failed FDIC covered institution, your investment is guaranteed up to a combined limit of $250,000.

NONE OF THE FOLLOWING ARE COVERED BY FDIC:

- Stocks
- Bonds (government, corporate and municipals)
- Mutual funds

- Insurance products
- Money market mutual funds
- Safety deposit boxes

Maximizing FDIC Protection

Should you have more than $250,000 in cash accounts, there are several ways to increase your FDIC coverage. First, the $250,000 limit is for each bank meaning that you could open accounts at a multitude of banks in order to increase coverage if needed. Should you prefer working with a single institution, there are ways to increase your coverage through different titling of assets.

EXAMPLE OF FDIC COVERAGE FOR A SINGLE INSTITUTION:

Husband individual account $250,000

+ Husband IRA account $250,000

+ Husband & wife joint account $250,000

+ Wife individual account $250,000

+ Wife IRA account $250,000

= Combined FDIC insurance of $1,250,000

RULE OF THUMB:
Never leave sums of cash in an account that are above FDIC coverage limits. This is too risky a proposition given the options available to investors.

THE SECURITIES INVESTORS PROTECTION CORP. (SIPC)

Not to be confused with FDIC, SIPC is a completely separate form of insurance for investors that is provided for brokerage accounts. SIPC aids customers of failed brokerage firms should their assets go missing from accounts. SIPC coverage is up to $500,000 per customer, which includes $250,000 in cash. Should investment fraud occur, SIPC typically will not provide insurance.

BONDS

Entities (both public and private) often decide they need financing for operations. Instead of going through a bank, an entity might look to the bond market.

A bond (also known as fixed income) is an investment that provides a reliable investment return via fixed periodic payments and the return of principal upon maturity. Essentially, it is an IOU. Unlike a variable-income security where payments change, the payments of a bond are typically known in advance.

Bond Term	Definitions
Face Value	Also referred to as par, face value is the amount a bond is initially sold and will return at maturity.
Coupon Rate	The stated rate of interest on an issued bond.
Maturity Date	The date which the bond will stop accruing interest and return principal.
Credit Rating	Many issuers will have their debt rated by a major credit rating agency which assesses the credit worthiness of a corporation's or government's debt issuance.
Call Features	Some bonds have specified dates on which the issuer can call or redeem the bond earlier than its stated maturity date.
Current Yield	The rate of interest paid by a bond at a current price.
Yield to Maturity	The total rate of return for a bond if held to maturity.
Yield to Worst	The worst possible return a bond can yield.
Insured	Some bonds (mainly municipals) may be insured by an insurance company against default.

Advantages of Bonds?

- – Steady and predictable income

- – Diversification

- – Lower volatility than stocks

- – Capital preservation

- – Absolute return

- – Potential tax advantages

DID YOU KNOW?

Long-term government bonds outperformed the stock market for the 30 years preceding 2012. These bonds gained 11.5% annually versus the 10.8% increase in the S&P 500.

Risks to Bonds

Just because bonds are guaranteed sources of income, this doesn't mean they are risk free. First of all, the guarantee on your interest and principal are only as good as the issuing entity. The risk doesn't stop there either, as investors can be potentially subject to interest rate risks as well. Interest rate changes can make your bond look better or worse, thus causing a change in value.

RULE OF THUMB

There is an inverse relationship between interest rates and bond prices. If interest rates are rising then typically bond prices are falling and vice versa.

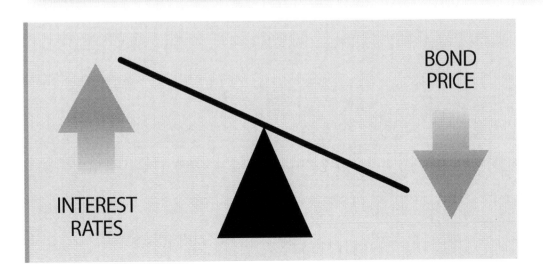

Bond Credit Ratings

Many bond issuers pay fees to credit rating agencies for ratings on bond issuances. These ratings give the public a simple way to assess the credit worthiness of a bond and potentially make bond issuances more marketable. The three largest credit rating agencies are Moody's, S&P, and Fitch.

CREDIT RATINGS

		Moody's	Standard & Poor's	Fitch
INVESTMENT GRADE	STRONGEST	Aaa	AAA	AAA
		Aa	AA	AA
		A	A	A
		Baa	BBB	BBB
NON-INVESTMENT GRADE		Ba	BB	BB
		B	B	B
		Caa	CCC	CCC
		Ca	CC	CC
	WEAKEST	C	C	C
		C	D	D

* These credit ratings are reflective of obligations with long-term maturities.

DID YOU KNOW?

In 2011, the US lost its Triple A rating with Standard & Poors for the first time.

Investment Grade Versus High-Yield

Any bonds that are rated below Triple-B are considered higher risk and referred to as high-yield or junk bonds. High-yield bonds typically have higher yields but also come with higher default rates. Historically, investment grade corporate bonds have had a default rate of 2%, but high-yield bond default rates can rise dramatically in tough economic times.

FITCH U.S. HIGH-YIELD DEFAULT INDEX

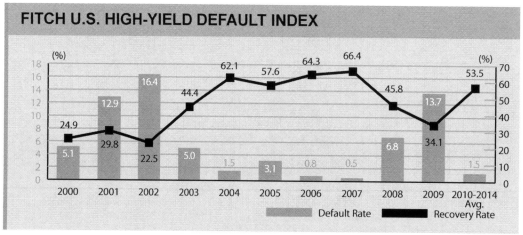

Source: Fitch Ratings, Credit Market Research: Fitch U.S. High-Yield Default Insight – April 2011; May 12, 2011

CALCULATING YIELD

Current Yield

On most bonds, the stated coupon rate of interest never changes. Many bonds trade on secondary exchanges, and because of this, the price for the bond is dictated by the market and interest rate environment. The current yield is the actual yield realized by an investor based on the purchase price of the bond.

FORMULA: **BOND COUPON ÷ BOND PRICE = CURRENT YIELD**

CURRENT YIELD EXAMPLE			
Purchased at:	**Price**	**Annual Interest**	**Current Yield**
Discount	$900	$80 (8% coupon)	8.88%
Par	$1000	$80 (8% coupon)	8%
Premium	$1100	$80 (8% coupon)	7.27%

Yield to Maturity

The yield to maturity (YTM) is the total return earned on a bond if it is held to maturity. YTM takes into consideration the current yield received plus the return on the bond generated by it returning to par value.

Formula: Current Yield + (Bond Premium/Discount ÷ Years to Maturity) = YTM

Example: 10 Year Bond Purchased at $1,100 (10% Premium) with 8% Coupon
7.27% (Current Yield) + (-10%(Premium Loss) ÷ 10 (Years)) = 6.27% YTM

Corporate Bonds

Corporations issue bonds in order to raise cash for financing business operations. These bonds pay interest that is fully taxable, and they typically have higher default rates and higher yields than government issued bonds.

Categories	
Asset-Backed	Secured by physical assets or collateral
Debentures	Unsecured loans
Convertible	A bond that can be converted into stock at a later date at a specified price

Corporate Bond Defaults

What happens if you hold a bond in a company that files for bankruptcy protection? One of the advantages of being a bond investor is that you are in a senior position to equity holders. Unlike stockholders, typically bond investors recover value at the end of bankruptcy. The potential recovery rate for a bond will depend heavily on the financial condition of the issuing entity and the entity's industry.

Bond defaults most often occur in high-yield bonds. In these more speculative securities, the average bond recovery rate was 48% in the past decade between 2001-2010 according to Fitch.

RULE OF THUMB

Capital intensive industries (miners or manufacturers) typically have better recovery rates than service based industries (banks or insurers). For example, when Lehman Brothers filed bankruptcy, its bond recovery rate was a paltry 8.625% (2008 Risk Magazine).

Municipal Bonds

Many state and local government organizations issue bonds. These bonds are generally federal tax-exempt, and if you purchase a bond issued by the state in which you live, it is usually state tax-exempt as well.

Categories	
Revenue Bonds	Backed by the earnings of a specific project the bond is financing (example: a toll road)
General Obligation Bonds (GO)	Backed by the full faith and credit of the issuer

RULE OF THUMB

Municipal bonds issued by U.S. territories like Puerto Rico are exempt from federal and state income tax regardless of your state of residency.

Effect of Federal Income Taxes on the Yields of Tax-Exempt and Taxable Instruments		
	4% Tax-Exempt	**6% Taxable**
Cash investment	$30,000	$30,000
Annual interest	$1,200	$1,800
Federal income tax in the 33% marginal bracket	$0	$594
Net return after taxes	$1,200	$1,206
Yield on investment after taxes	4.0%	4.02%

Build America Bonds

The American Recovery and Reinvestment Act of 2009 ushered in a new type of municipal bond called Build America Bonds. These bonds are taxable and are, therefore, appropriate for tax deferred accounts such as IRAs. The other aspect unique to Build America Bonds is that the federal government subsidizes 35% of the interest for the issuer. Issuance of these bonds ended in 2010, but due to long maturities, these bonds will trade in secondary markets for decades to come.

U.S. Government Bonds

The federal government and its many different agencies issue a number of different fixed income securities that are backed by the credit of the United States. Because of this backing, these securities generally have relatively low yields.

Bond Category	Details
U.S. Treasuries	– Broken down into bills, notes and bonds depending on length of maturity – Subject to federal tax but not state or local income tax
Treasury Inflation Protected Securities	– (TIPS) Interest and redemption payments are tied to inflation
Agency Bonds	– Issued by U.S. Agencies like Fannie Mae, Freddie Mac, Sallie Mae and the Federal Home Loan Banks – No preferential tax treatment
Savings Bonds	– Sold as Series EE and I-Bonds – EE bonds are exempt from state and local income tax – Now only sold through treasury.gov

International Bonds

International bonds are issued in foreign countries and are typically issued in the foreign country's currency. Like domestic bonds, they pay interest at specific intervals and pay the principal amount back to the bond's buyer at maturity. These bonds are also issued by both corporations and governments just like domestic bonds.

One important difference for investors to be aware of in international bonds is currency exchange rate risk. The changes in currency exchange rates can either decrease or enhance your returns in foreign denominated bonds.

OWNING INVESTMENTS

Stocks

A stock is a security that signifies ownership in a corporation and represents a claim on a portion of the company's assets and earnings. As a part owner in a company, you have a vested interest in that company. Characteristics of stock ownership are:

– Gains or loss in the price of the stock

– Potential dividends from company profits

– Voting rights

– No tax liability on appreciation until the stock is sold

Categorizing Stocks

There are thousands of publicly traded stocks and many different ways to categorize them. One of the more popular categorizations is the Morningstar Style Box™, which breaks stocks down by growth characteristics and market capitalization.

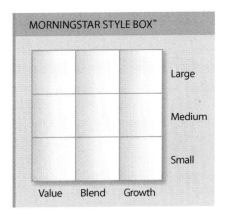

Market Capitalization

Another way to categorize investments is by the size of the corporation. If you multiply the number of shares outstanding in a company (the "float") times its current share price, you get the total value of the company. This is known as a company's market cap. A typical breakdown of market cap is:

Large Cap	Company value greater than $10 billion (Apple, Verizon, Wal-Mart)
Mid Cap	Company value between $2 billion and $10 billion (Goodyear Tire, Under Armour)
Small Cap	Company value less than $2 billion (Denny's, TiVo)

*Company examples as of December 2017

Growth Versus Value

Growth and value investing are two very different mind sets. Value investors are primarily concerned with the current state and valuation of a company. They look for stocks that are trading for less than their apparent worth based on current company revenue and profit.

However, growth investors focus on the future potential of a company and place much less emphasis on the company's present revenue and profitability. Unlike value investors, growth investors buy companies that are trading higher than their current intrinsic worth with the belief that the companies' intrinsic worth will grow and therefore exceed their current valuations.

Sectors

Companies can also be categorized by the industry they represent. Stocks in similar industries have a tendency to move in tandem and are highly correlated.

- Financials (JP Morgan)
- Information Technology (Microsoft)
- Health Care (Pfizer)
- Telecommunications (AT&T)
- Energy (Exxon)

- Utilities (Duke Energy)
- Consumer Discretionary (Target)
- Industrials (General Electric)
- Consumer Staples (Proctor & Gamble)
- Materials (Alcoa)

Preferred Stock

The most familiar type of stock are aptly named as "common" stocks. Another category of stock ownership exists that is called "preferred". Preferred shares are considered to be a hybrid of both stocks and bonds since they have characteristics of both.

TYPICAL CHARACTERISTICS OF PREFERRED STOCKS

- Guaranteed dividend payments
- No voting rights
- Typically less volatile
- Traded more infrequently than common stocks
- Priority over common stockholders with regard to dividends and bankruptcy

RULE OF THUMB

Historically, the financial sector has been the largest issuer of preferred stock.

POOLED INVESTING

Many times, investors choose to pool their funds with other investors. By doing so, they may be able to achieve greater diversification than they could on their own. Additionally, they also may be able to get professional management in the process.

Mutual Funds

Launched in 1928, mutual funds are one of the oldest and largest forms of pooled investments. A mutual fund is an open-end investment company that pools and invests money for investors. A share in a mutual fund represents a proportionate ownership share in the total fund holdings.

CHARACTERISTICS OF MUTUAL FUNDS

– Low minimum investments

– Daily liquidity at the close of markets

– Variety of investment strategies (there are over 10,000 mutual funds)

– Can invest in most assets such as cash, bonds and stocks

– No control over security purchases in the fund

– Low level of transparency in fund investments

Mutual Fund Fees

It costs money to operate mutual funds, and investors should be aware that different mutual funds can have vastly different internal fees. All mutual funds have an expense ratio. This ratio may be comprised of the following:

– Management fee (all funds)

– Operating expense (all funds)

– Distribution or 12b-1 Fees (most funds)

– Sales loads (load funds only)

SALES LOADS

Some share classes of mutual funds cost nothing to purchase up front. These are typically referred to as "no-load" funds. In contrast, load funds generally require a payment to the selling brokerage in the form of either a front or back-end sales load. Some investment platforms, such as a 401(k), have access to load funds that are "load waived."

A-Shares	Have the lowest ongoing expense but have an up-front sales load of around 5%
B-Shares	Higher ongoing expenses but convert to A-Shares after 7 to 10 years. Also has a deferred sales load fee if sold before 7 years
C-Shares	Considered a "level" load, meaning it always has higher ongoing expenses but no penalty if sold after 12 months

RULE OF THUMB

All things being equal, the mutual fund with the lowest fee is typically your best bet.

EXCHANGE-TRADED FUNDS (ETF)

ETFs are similar to mutual funds in that they pool investor funds and invest in a basket of securities. They were first introduced in 1992, and their popularity has grown substantially over the past two decades. They differ from mutual funds in several ways:

- Trade intra-day like a stock

- Greater transparency

- Trading prices can deviate from the net asset value (NAV) of the underlying investments

- No minimum investments

- Access to leveraged and inverse strategies

UNIT INVESTMENT TRUSTS (UIT)

A UIT is an investment company that offers a fixed, unmanaged portfolio, generally of stocks and bonds, as redeemable "units" to investors. Unlike mutual funds and ETFs, a UIT is designed to be in existence for a specific amount of time, at which point it will liquidate. UITs are designed to provide capital appreciation and/or dividend income. With the growth of ETFs over the past decade, the utilization of UITs by investors have shrunk significantly.

HEDGE FUNDS

Hedge funds are usually set up as private investment partnerships that are open to a limited number of investors and require a large initial minimum investment. A hedge fund is nothing more than an investment vehicle just like a mutual fund or ETF. However, they differ in some very important ways:

- Greater access to more advanced strategies

- Access to non-publicly traded investments

- Lock-up periods

- Large minimums

- Less regulation and transparency

- Incentive fees based on investment performance

- Issue schedule K-1 partnership tax statements

RULE OF THUMB

An investor can only purchase hedge funds (Regulation D Private Securities) if he is classified as an accredited investor. An accredited investor is an investor with a minimum net worth of US$1 million or, alternatively, a minimum income of US$200,000 ($300,000 joint income) in each of the last two years and a reasonable expectation of reaching the same income level in the current year. For banks and corporate entities, the minimum net worth is US$5 million in invested assets.

ALTERNATIVE INVESTMENTS

Many types of investments do not broadly fit into the categories of cash, stocks and bonds. These investments are many times referred to as "alternative investments." The alternative investment space has been dominated by hedge funds; however, it is possible to get exposure to this investment class through mutual funds and ETFs. Some categories of investments that are considered alternative investments are:

- Real estate

- Commodities (gold, silver, corn)

- Futures contracts

- Options (calls and puts)

- Credit default swaps (CDS)

- Real assets (timber, mines)

- Absolute return (short/long strategies)

Popularity in the alternative investment space has grown over the past two decades due to a perceived greater access to diversification and returns that are non-correlated to the stock market. A great example of this shift has been seen in the Harvard Endowment. The investment strategy deployed by them has greatly shifted over the past 30 years from what used to be a "traditional" portfolio of stocks and bonds.

HARVARD ENDOWMENT ALLOCATION

Asset Class	1980	1984	1988	1995	1999	2002	2008	2013	2016
Domestic Equity	66%	47%	46%	38%	24%	15%	12%	11%	11%
Foreign Equity	0%	0%	0%	20%	24%	15%	12%	11%	18%
Private Equity	0%	7%	12%	12%	12%	13%	11%	16%	20%
Real Assets	0%	3%	5%	15%	17%	29%	26%	25%	24%
Fixed Income	34%	43%	37%	17%	17%	16%	15%	9%	13%
Alternative	0%	0%	0%	0%	6%	12%	24%	28%	14%

Source: Harvard University, Annual Report of the Harvard Management Company

CHAPTER 5:

INVESTMENT STRATEGY

PREPARING FOR RETIREMENT

A COMPREHENSIVE GUIDE TO FINANCIAL PLANNING

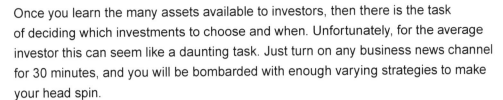

INVESTMENT STRATEGIES

Once you learn the many assets available to investors, then there is the task of deciding which investments to choose and when. Unfortunately, for the average investor this can seem like a daunting task. Just turn on any business news channel for 30 minutes, and you will be bombarded with enough varying strategies to make your head spin.

Thankfully, through all the noise that exists for investors, there are some tried and true investment strategies:

- Asset allocation & diversification

- Rebalancing

- Strategic asset allocations

-Tactical asset allocations

- Active versus passive investing

- Fundamental versus technical analysis

- Maturity laddering

- Long versus short

- Dollar cost averaging

The investment strategy utilized in your retirement planning should have an investment target that is in line with the assumptions used within your financial plan. If your financial plan assumes returns of 10% going forward, then obviously this type of return will be impossible without deploying a fairly aggressive strategy. Your investment strategy should always be in line with your underlying investment goals and risk tolerance.

RULE OF THUMB
Buy low, sell high! It's that simple!

INVESTMENT RISKS

Market Risk

When investing, there is always a risk that you will experience a loss of principal. As markets fluctuate there could be periods of time where your portfolio loses a significant amount of value. During times when the stock market is down 20% or more it is considered a "bear market."

While you are saving for retirement, a bear market can actually be advantageous because you are buying securities at lower prices. However, once you are no longer adding to savings and instead depleting them, a bear market can be much more damaging to your retirement plans.

How Many Years to Recover from Bear Markets?

Bear Market	Duration (Months)	% Decline	Years Needed to Break Even
Sept '29 June '32	33	86.7%	25.2
July '33 - Mar '35	20	33.9%	2.3
Mar '37 - Mar '38	12	54.5%	8.8
Nov '38 - Apr '42	41	45.8%	6.4
May '46 - Mar '48	22	28.1%	4.1
Aug '56 - Oct '57	14	21.6%	2.1
Dec '61 - June '62	6	28.0%	1.8
Feb '66 - Oct '66	8	22.2%	1.4
Nov '68 - May '70	18	36.1%	3.3
Jan '73 - Oct '74	21	48.2%	7.6
Nov '80 - Aug '82	21	27.1%	2.1
Aug '87 - Dec '87	4	33.5%	1.9
July '90 - Oct '90	3	19.9%	0.6
Mar '00 - Mar '03	35	49.2%	4.7
Oct '07 - Mar '09	18	56.2%	5.5
Averages	18.4	39.4%	5.2

Source – S&P 500 Data

ASSET ALLOCATION AND DIVERSIFICATION

As the old saying goes, "There is no such thing as a free lunch." When it comes to investing, diversification is as close as it gets to a free lunch. By investing in a broad array of assets, an investor can potentially lower the volatility and risk in a portfolio. The asset allocation you choose can be the difference in whether or not your financial plan will be successful in the long run.

The study of asset allocation began with Modern Portfolio Theory in 1952. In its most basic form, Modern Portfolio Theory attempts to maximize the expected return in a portfolio for a given amount of portfolio risk, or equivalently minimize risk for a given level of expected return, by carefully choosing the proportions of various assets.

Consider the following asset allocations, all of which increase the level of equities utilized as the aggressiveness of a portfolio increases. A properly diversified portfolio should generate a certain amount of return for each additional unit of risk being taken.

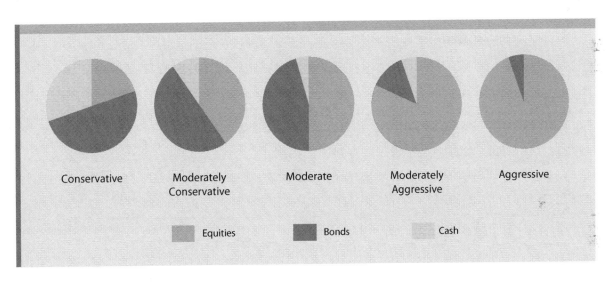

| Conservative | Moderately Conservative | Moderate | Moderately Aggressive | Aggressive |

Equities   Bonds   Cash

How Important is Asset Allocation?

Asset allocation is the most important component of a portfolio; thus, the most time should be spent on developing it properly.

According to a 1986 study titled "Determinants of Portfolio Performance," over 90% of the return of your portfolio will be dictated by the asset allocation utilized. The remaining factors that will affect returns are things such as security selection and market timing. While many investors spend long hours fine tuning stock picks and trying to time the markets, that time would most likely be better spent fine tuning their asset allocation instead.

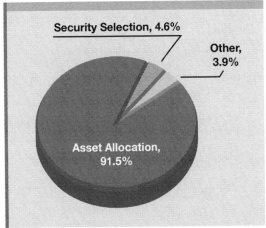

Security Selection, 4.6%
Other, 3.9%
Asset Allocation, 91.5%

REBALANCING

Since asset allocation is so important, it is equally important to make sure that your allocation is being properly maintained over time. In the long-term, it is assumed that riskier assets in a portfolio will outperform less risky assets. Therefore, these assets will grow to be a larger piece of the allocation pie.

Portfolio rebalancing is how you keep your initial target allocation in tact. Rebalancing entails selling off the highest performing assets that have grown too large due to outperformance relative to other assets. While it might seem counterintuitive to sell the assets doing the best in your portfolio, you must remember that this discipline keeps the risk/return profile of your portfolio in tact. As an investor you want to be the one dictating your asset allocation, not the markets.

RULE OF THUMB

Rebalancing needs to be done at least annually, but doing it more than quarterly can sometimes become counter productive.

Effects of Not Rebalancing

Asset	Starting Value	Starting % of Portfolio	Annual Return	Ending Value	Ending % of Portfolio
Stocks	$200,000	67%	25%	$250,000	71%
Bonds	$100,000	33%	2%	$102,000	29%

In this example, the initial allocations in this portfolio have shifted 4% after just one year of returns. Without rebalancing for several years, it's not unusual for a portfolio to shift 10-20% from its original target allocation.

Strategic Versus Tactical Asset Allocation

Strategic asset allocation calls for setting target allocations and then periodically rebalancing the portfolio back to those targets as investment returns skew the original asset allocation percentages. Tactical asset allocation allows for a range on target allocations (40-60% equities, for example). A tactical investor will modify their allocations to an asset class depending on whether they are bullish or bearish on that asset.

Example: A tactical investor is aggressive and usually maintains a target equity allocation of 80% equities. However, they are currently bearish on the stock market and are utilizing only a 60% allocation to equities.

PASSIVE VERSUS ACTIVE INVESTING

When deciding when to rebalance your portfolio, you must consider whether or not you are going to try to time markets at a point potentially advantageous for your returns. This brings up the subject of passive versus active investing.

Passive investing operates on the assumption that investors are incapable of market timing or picking individual investments that will outperform the underlying indexes.

Active investing assumes that through research and market timing you can outperform the underlying indexes.

	Advantages	Disadvantages
Passive Investing	– Lower fees – Easy to pick index funds – Funds never close	– Impossible to outperform
Active Investing	– Potential to outperform – Potential to lower risk	– Potential to underperform – Higher fees – Good managers close funds – More time consuming

How to Decide Between Passive and Active Funds

Some schools of thought insist that passive investing is the only way you should choose to invest because of the long-term benefits of lower fees. However, there are other investors who prefer the potential outperformance of active investing. There are merits to both strategies, and it's possible to use both styles in portfolio creation. Some asset classes lend themselves to active management better than others.

If you can find investment managers with a proven track record of success, then it may be to your advantage to pay greater fees in order to obtain a potentially higher return. However, if you have searched through fund managers and no such manager can be found in a given sector, you're probably better off investing passively through index funds.

TYPES OF ANALYSIS USED IN ACTIVE INVESTING

Fundamental Analysis

Fundamental analysis of a business involves analyzing the financial statements and the overall health of a corporation. This could involve assessing its products, management, and competitive advantages. When analyzing a business you must not just focus on the single business but also their competitors. When applied to broader investments, such as an index, it focuses on things such as the overall state of the economy and interest rates.

Technical Analysis

Technical analysis in its purest form focuses solely on charts and ignores the underlying fundamentals of the investment. Technical analysts use different indicators that they feel predict future market performance.

It's important to consider fundamental and technical analysis in your investment strategy. Just because you believe in only one doesn't mean the markets can't be affected by the other.

RULE OF THUMB

Stock charts change on a daily basis, but very little changes on a week to week basis in large corporations. So, the shorter the term of your investment, the more important technical analysis becomes in your decision making.

Laddering Maturities

Laddering involves staggering the maturities of fixed income investments. This strategy can lower risk by avoiding the risk of reinvesting a large portion of assets in an unfavorable financial environment. It also limits the downside should you have a single issuer default.

Example Bond Ladder

Maturity	Rate	Amount
1 Year	1%	$10,000
3 Years	2.5%	$10,000
5 Years	3.5%	$10,000
10 Years	4%	$10,000
15 Years	5%	$10,000

Portfolio Averages: 6.8 Year Maturity and 3.2% Yield

Dollar Cost Averaging

Dollar cost averaging is the strategy of investing equal amounts of money over certain intervals of time. By investing over a period of time one can effectively take market timing out of the investing equation.

Dollar cost averaging can be especially effective in retirement planning. Because it is generally done over a 30 year period or longer, it allows you to take greater risk with your assets. During down stock market periods, your dollars purchasing equities will have greater purchasing power due to lower stock prices.

RULE OF THUMB

In retirement, you'll no longer have the effects of dollar cost averaging in your favor, so you may need to take less risk with your assets.

Shorting

Shorting stock is the practice of borrowing stock (typically through a broker) to sell now, with the hope of purchasing it back at a later date at a lower price. When you own stock, you are considered to be "long," while the practice of selling a stock to open a position is considered being "short."

Shorting stock is one of a handful of methods to profit in a down market. However, since the general long-term trend of stock markets is upwards, it makes shorting stock very difficult as a sustainable strategy. Additionally, unlike owning stock where your downside loss is limited (100% maximum loss), short positions are theoretically subject to unlimited losses when shorting. For these reasons, a "short" strategy should be limited to only a small percentage of a total portfolio.

Beware! You may not be able to hold a short position forever at your brokerage firm. Shares are only allowed to be shorted if your brokerage firm has the ability to borrow the shares. Should shares become unavailable, you can potentially be forced to buy back your short position at an inopportune time, leading to what is known as a "short squeeze."

Shorting Stock Example

An investor sells short 100 Shares of ABC at $25 and purchases it back 6 months later at $20 for a $5 gain. The investor books a gain of $500. If ABC stock paid any dividends over this 6 month period, the investor would owe the dividend amount to the lender as well.

MEASURING RISK

Everyone knows that it is important to measure the performance of your investments. However, many people overlook the amount of risk they're taking to obtain those returns. This is partially because risk measurements can be difficult to calculate for the average investor and typically takes advanced software to compute.

Correlation – The statistical measurement of how two securities move in relation to each other is considered their correlation. Correlation is measured between -1 to 1. A correlation of 1 means two securities move in perfect lockstep over a given time period, and a correlation of -1 means two securities move in perfectly opposite directions. If correlation is 0 then there is no relation between the movement in two securities.

10 Year Investment Correlation Matrix

	Large Cap Growth	Small Cap Growth	Non-US Equities	REITs	Com-modities	High-Yield Bonds	Invest-ment Grade Bonds
Large Cap Growth	1.00						
Small Cap Growth	0.86	1.00					
Non-US Equities	0.58	0.54	1.00				
REITs	0.44	0.54	0.39	1.00			
Commodities	0.12	0.16	0.18	0.16	1.00		
High-Yield Bonds	0.52	0.58	0.40	0.50	0.04	1.00	
Investment Grade Bonds	0.19	0.10	0.17	0.16	-0.10	0.38	1.00

Source: Morningstar Correlation Matrix, 2018

Beta – Beta is a measurement of volatility for an individual security or a portfolio. Generally in investing, beta is calculated in reference to the S&P 500, which is indexed with a beta of 1.0. If a security has a beta less than 1.0 then that security is considered less volatile than the overall stock market. A security with a beta greater than 1.0 is more volatile than the overall stock market.

Standard Deviation – Standard deviation is a measure of the dispersion of a set of data from its average. The greater the dispersion from the mean, the higher the standard deviation. In investing, standard deviation is applied to the annual rate of return to measure volatility. One can measure a portfolio's standard deviation to the S&P 500 in a similar way as Beta. If a portfolio has a standard deviation lower than the S&P 500's standard deviation, it is considered to have lower risk and volatility. The opposite is true for a standard deviation higher than the S&P 500. However, unlike Beta, the standard deviation of the S&P 500 is continually changing depending on the overall volatility of the markets during a given time period.

Alpha – Alpha is a way of measuring a portfolio's effectiveness relative to the amount of risk taken. A positive Alpha number signifies outperformance on a relative basis in a portfolio while a negative number signifies underperformance.

BEHAVIORAL RISK

Does emotion play an important part in your investment decisions? Several Nobel Prize award winners in economics have studied investor psychology and the effect it has on investment returns. The overwhelming consensus of the data confirms that greater emotion in investing decisions has a strongly negative effect on investment performance.

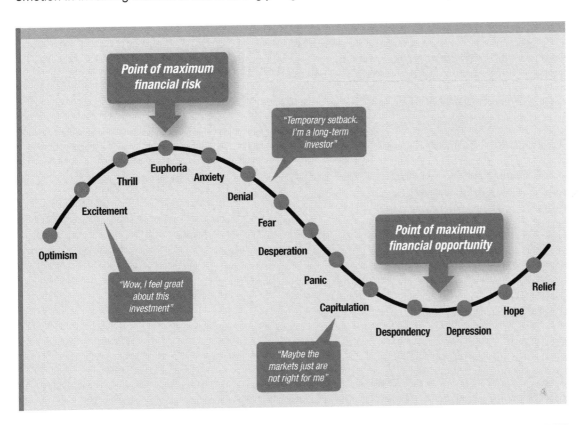

QUESTIONS TO ASK YOURSELF:

– Do you become more or less aggressive during market downturns?

– Do you dwell on missed investment opportunities?

– Do you get emotionally attached to investments?

– Do you refuse to sell a "loser"?

– Are you prone to chasing performance?

It is natural for investors to experience highs and lows in conjunction with market cycles. However, if you are prone to making investment decisions based on these feelings, your investment performance may suffer. After all, the old saying goes, "Buy low, sell high." If you are trigger happy to sell positions during a sell-off then you may want to consider a less aggressive investment allocation.

EFFICIENT FRONTIER

The different measurements of risk are utilized to build efficient portfolios. An efficient portfolio is one that maximizes potential returns for the amount of risk currently being utilized. For example, a portfolio that is 100% fixed income is not considered a perfectly efficient portfolio. Because of the benefits of diversification, it is actually possible to use a 20% equities and 80% fixed income portfolio to realize greater returns and lower the overall level of risk.

As you move farther out on the efficient frontier in hopes of higher returns, eventually a portfolio begins to have marginal increases in return for every unit of additional risk. At some point, it is possible to be taking on additional investment risk with no real increase in expected returns. This is considered taking risk for the sake of risk and is an ineffective long-term investment strategy.

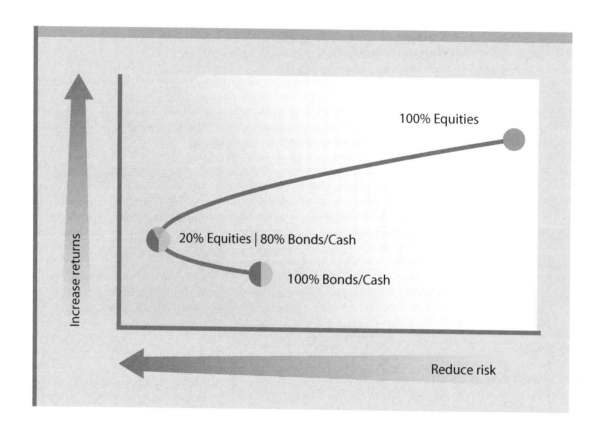

RULE OF THUMB:

A popular rule of thumb is that the equities percentage in your portfolio should be equal to 100 minus your age. So, if you are 60 you should be in 40% stocks (100 – 60 = 40%) with the remainder in fixed income.

Diversification In Action

Assume you retired on 12/31/2004 with a $1 million nest egg plus social security to fulfill your retirement income needs. Your savvy advisor has informed you that based on inflation, longevity, and investment returns, a withdrawal rate of 4% or $40,000 would be a historically safe amount to pull annually from your portfolio. Accordingly, you begin taking distributions at the end of each year, adjusting the initial $40,000 amount higher by 2% each year to account for the decreasing purchase power associated with inflation.

10 Year Annual Returns for S&P 500 and Barclays Bond Index											
Index	2005	2006	2007	2008	2009	2010	2011	2012	2013	2014	Avg.
S&P 500	3.0%	13.6%	3.5%	-38%	23.5%	12.8%	0.0%	13.4%	29.6%	11.4%	7.2%
Bond	-4.5%	6.6%	9.5%	4.8%	6.9%	5.5%	5.6%	4.3%	-2.6%	6.0%	4.2%
50/50 Mix	-0.7%	10.1%	6.5%	-17%	15.2%	9.2%	2.8%	8.9%	13.5%	8.7%	5.7%

$1,000,000 Portfolio with 4% Annual Withdrawal, 2% Inflation								
100% S&P 500			100% Bonds			50/50 Mix		
Year	Return	Year End Total	Year	Return	Year End Total	Year	Return	Year End Total
2005	3.00%	$990,000	2005	-4.49%	$915,100	2005	-0.7%	$952,550
2006	13.62%	$1,084,038	2006	6.64%	$935,063	2006	10.1%	$1,008,243
2007	3.53%	$1,080,689	2007	9.48%	$982,091	2007	6.5%	$1,032,214
2008	-38.49%	$622,283	2008	4.79%	$986,684	2008	-16.9%	$815,837
2009	23.45%	$724,911	2009	6.93%	$1,011,764	2009	15.2%	$896,466
2010	12.78%	$773,392	2010	5.54%	$1,023,653	2010	9.2%	$934,419
2011	0%	$728,345	2011	5.64%	$1,036,340	2011	2.8%	$915,723
2012	13.41%	$780,069	2012	4.32%	$1,035,163	2012	8.9%	$950,954
2013	29.60%	$964,103	2013	-2.60%	$961,382	2013	13.5%	$1,032,467
2014	11.39%	$1,026,111	2014	5.97%	$970,973	2014	8.7%	$1,074,281

Remarkably, even though the S&P 500 annualized at 7.2% over this 10 year period, a 50/50 portfolio actually outperformed an all stock portfolio with $1,074,281 at the end of the 10 years. This is directly due to avoiding the entire brunt of the 2008 38% market loss for an all stock portfolio while also taking portfolio distributions. While this real world example only uses two asset classes, it clearly shows the value of diversification.

CHAPTER 6:

ACCUMULATION

PREPARING FOR RETIREMENT
A Comprehensive Guide to Financial Planning

ACCUMULATION

The last several decades have seen a huge shift in the way investors save and prepare for retirement. As corporations have phased out defined benefit plans, like pensions, it has now become largely the responsibility of the employee to save for retirement. With the burden of retirement saving out of the hands of employers, it's important for savers to know the most efficient route to save and grow their assets. While investing in an ordinary, taxable account is always available, there are other tax advantaged forms to consider as well.

When building a successful accumulation strategy, it's important to realize that just like the rest of financial planning, this is not a one step process. A successful strategy will focus on long-term, annual contributions. The earlier you start, the better.

DEFINED BENEFIT PLANS

Better known as pensions, defined benefit plans have represented a significant portion of retirement savings for workers over the past century. Under a defined benefit plan agreement, an employer funds and manages a group pension fund in order to provide workers a guaranteed stream of income for life upon retirement.

Because pension plans guarantee a certain amount of income to retirees, the sponsors of these plans are on the hook for properly funding and investing the assets over time. Because of this risk, many employers, especially those in the private sector, have discontinued pension plans.

For most employees, there is little that needs to be done in regards to saving money within a pension. Either your employer has a plan or they don't. However, some employers now offer new employees the option of whether to fund a defined benefit or defined contribution plan.

If you are a business owner, you will have the decision of whether or not to put in place a defined benefit plan. During the consideration process, a business owner should keep in mind that they'll potentially be required to provide similar benefits to all employees, not just themselves. However, in the right situation a business owner has the possibility to turn huge annual deferrals into a defined benefit plan.

RULE OF THUMB
Unless you plan on working for an employer 10 years or more, you will most likely be better off funding a defined contribution plan over a pension plan option.

DEFINED CONTRIBUTION PLANS

Defined contribution plans are retirement saving plans that are sponsored by an employer. Whereas pensions have lost their popularity over the past few decades, defined contribution plans have come in as their replacement.

Unlike a pension that guarantees a set benefit upon retirement, a defined contribution plan only provides a set amount (such as a match) that an employer will contribute to an employee's balance. There are numerous types of defined benefit plans, and some employers may offer multiple plans. While each plan differs in details, most share some common characteristics:

- Individual accounts with various investment options
- Employee contributions are done via payroll deductions and are pre-tax
- Employee contributions vest immediately
- Employer contributions may have vesting schedules
- Beneficiary designations are available
- Potential to take loans if available within plan
- Catch up contributions for those over age 50

401(k)

One of the most common savings plans today is the 401(k) plan. It is named after the section of the Internal Revenue code that refers to it. Plan benefits from employer to employer can vary greatly. However, all plans allow for employees to defer up to $18,500 annually and up to $24,500 for those over age 50 (these amounts are indexed periodically for inflation).

401(k) plans are not limited to larger size businesses. A business with one employee can open what is called a single person 401(k). Such a plan allows for significant plan contributions with minimal administration costs.

403(b)

The 403(b) plan works very similarly to the 401(k). The primary difference in the plans is that 403(b) plans are only available to government and non-profit entities. Beyond that there is currently little difference between the 403(b) and 401(k) from an employee standpoint, as they share the same contribution maximums.

Currently, there is a 403(b) additional lifetime catch-up which allows participants with more than 15 years of service who are older than 50 years of age to contribute an additional $3,000 per year. The maximum lifetime additional catch-up is $15,000.

457

457 plans work similarly to the 401(k) and 403(b) and are available only to public sector employees. In 2018, $18,500 can be contributed to a 457 plan annually in addition to fully funding a 401(k) or 403(b). Another $6,000 is allowed in catch-up contributions for those over age 50.

If multiple plans are available, participants may maximize contributions to both a 401(k) or 403(b) and their 457 plan. For a public employee who has a higher earning spouse, this is a great way to defer a large portion of one's salary into retirement savings.

RULE OF THUMB

Always make sure to take full advantage of any company match offered by your employer. Investment returns may not be guaranteed, but you can always bank on instant growth via matching.

SIMPLE IRA

The SIMPLE IRA (Savings Incentive Match Plan for Employees) is limited to businesses with fewer than 100 employees. The maximum deferral contribution to a SIMPLE IRA in 2018 is $12,500 for those less than 50 years of age, and $15,500 for those greater than 50 ($3,000 catch-up).

One unique aspect to the SIMPLE IRA is that assets must be held for 2 years in order for assets to be eligible for rollover. Any distribution or rollover prior to the 2-year mark is subject to a 25% penalty.

Employers have little flexibility in determining matching options within a SIMPLE plan. They have the two following options:

A 2% non-elective employer contribution where eligible employees receive an employer contribution equal to 2% of their compensation (limited to $265,000 per year for 2015 and subject to cost-of-living adjustments for later years), regardless of whether they make their own contributions.

——— **OR** ———

A dollar-for-dollar match up to 3% of compensation where only the participating employees who have elected to make contributions will receive an employer contribution (i.e., the matching contribution).

SEP IRA

The SEP IRA (Simplified Employee Pension) is another plan designed for small businesses and the self-employed. In 2018, employee/employer contributions are capped at the lesser of $55,000, or 25% of employee compensation, or 20% of net earnings from self-employment with a maximum compensation of $275,000 per employee.

No catch-up provisions apply and loans are not available in the SEP IRA. If a self-employed individual has eligible employees, that employer is typically required to make contributions for those employees in order to utilize a SEP IRA.

Plan Administration Costs

Typically, the SIMPLE IRA and SEP IRA have the lowest administration costs for business owners because these plans are designed for small businesses and are not subject to the Employee Retirement Income Security Act (ERISA) or Department of Labor (DOL) oversight. 401(k) and 403(b) plans are subject to these guidelines and require extensive testing in order to be available.

Traditional 401(k) & 403(b) versus Roth 401(k) & 403(b)

Over the past decade many retirement plans have started offering employees the option between a traditional tax deferred plan and the new Roth option within the plan. The primary difference between these plans is that the Roth version provides no tax deferral up front for the employee, but the account grows tax free for life. In other words, the Roth is funded with after-tax dollars; therefore, distributions from the plan are not taxable.

RULE OF THUMB

Once you jump from the 12% to the 22% marginal tax bracket or higher it may make more sense to contribute to a traditional plan for the immediate tax deduction.

Employer Plan Investment Options

When contributing to an employer based plan, you may be limited in your investment options. ERISA regulations only require that a plan have 3 funds available for participants. Also, depending on your plan structure, you may not have a separate account for investing—meaning you could have zero input in your investments (similar to a pension plan).

Most employer based plans provide mutual fund options for investing and typically provide between 5 to 20 fund choices for investment. However, over the past decade, more investment options have become mainstream in the defined contribution space, and some plans can utilize ETFs or even individual stocks.

Individual Retirement Accounts (IRAs)

Employees are not required to save for retirement through an employer sponsored plan. Individual Retirement Accounts have been available since 1974 when they were enacted by ERISA. In 2018, IRA rules allow individuals to contribute up to $5,500 per year and an additional $1,000 in catch-up contributions for anyone over age 50. However, individuals are only eligible to contribute to an IRA to the extent of their earned income.

Example: If you work part-time and make $3,000, you are limited to $3,000 in IRA contributions.

Phase-Out Ranges For Deductibility Traditional IRA Contributions for 2018
Joint: $99,000 - $119,000 MAGI
Single: $63,000 - $73,000 MAGI

Roth IRA

The Roth IRA works similarly to the traditional IRA with two key differences. Contributions are not tax deductible; however, the funds grow tax-free for life. Additionally, unlike a traditional IRA, there are no required minimum distributions for Roth accounts.

Roth Contribution Phase-Out Ranges for 2018
Joint: $186,000 - $199,000 MAGI
Single: $120,000 - $135,000 MAGI

History of Traditional IRA & Roth Maximum Annual Contributions		
Year	IRA Maximum	Catch-Up
2008	$5,000	$1,000
2009	$5,000	$1,000
2010	$5,000	$1,000
2011	$5,000	$1,000
2012	$5,000	$1,000
2013	$5,500	$1,000
2014	$5,500	$1,000
2015	$5,500	$1,000
2016	$5,500	$1,000
2017	$5,500	$1,000
2018	$5,500	$1,000

The IRA maximum contributions and catch-up limits are indexed with inflation, so if you're looking to maximize contributions, make sure you stay up to date on the current limits.

Spousal IRAs

A non-working spouse can also contribute to an IRA if the person's spouse has earned income and if they fall below the contribution phase outs. A spousal IRA has the same contribution limits of $5,500 ($6,500 for those over age 50 for 2018).

Spousal Contribution Phase Out
2018: $189,000 - $199,000 MAGI

Married but Filing Separately

Most IRA contributions are extremely limited for individuals who are married and filing separately. Phase-out's for this situation typically start at $1 and phase out entirely at $10,000 in income.

Rollover IRAs

A rollover is when assets are moved from one qualified account to another. Done properly, a rollover will incur no tax ramifications. The most typical reason for a rollover is when assets are moved out of an employer based account into an individual IRA. This typically occurs on separation of service from an employer, but some plans allow for an in-service rollover after age 55.

Rollover Positives	Rollover Negatives
Greater control	Penalty free access at 59 ½ (Age 55 in 401(k))
More investment options	No loan availability
Account consolidation	Loses rollover designation if contributed to
Greater distribution options	
Can move back to employer plan	
Retains creditor protections	

Investment Options in Employer Plans Versus IRAs

While employer based plans might be limited to a handful of mutual funds, there is little limitation within IRAs. IRAs have access to a wide array of investment options.

Allowed in IRA	Not Allowed in IRA
Stocks	
Bonds	
Mutual Funds	Life Insurance
Annuities	Shorting Stock
ETFs	Naked Options
Options	
Hedge Funds	
Precious Metals	
Real Estate*	
Small Business*	

*Real estate and small business investment can only be completed through a proper intermediary and custodian specializing in this practice. Tax counsel should be consulted before investing qualified funds in such an intermediary.

Roth Conversions

The opportunity currently exists for any investor to convert funds in an IRA to a Roth IRA regardless of income. Income tax is due on any amount moved the year a Roth IRA conversion is completed.

Should I convert to a Roth?

There are a number of items to consider when converting to a Roth IRA. When deciding on a Roth conversion you'll have to consider the following:

1) Your current and expected future tax bracket

2) Time for compounded growth

3) Cash availability outside qualified accounts to pay conversion taxes

4) Desire to leave legacy assets to heirs that won't be subject to required minimum distributions

RULE OF THUMB

If completing a Roth IRA conversion, consider performing it at the beginning of the year. This extends the amount of time you have to pay the taxes, plus you'll have the opportunity to see market performance for the year. You may decide to reverse the conversion through a recharacterization if the account value decreases over the year.

Deferred Annuities

Annuities are another option for retirement savings thanks to their tax deferred growth. Unlike qualified accounts, there are no limits to the amount placed into a deferred annuity. Once an annuity is funded, it will grow tax free until the time at which assets are distributed outside of the annuity. There are no tax deductions available in the year in which a deferred annuity is funded.

Inherited IRAs

If you have an IRA that is not depleted before you die, it will be passed to your spouse, heirs or other beneficiaries. A beneficiary to an IRA will have 3 options:

Option 1 – The IRA may be cashed out in full with income taxes due on the proceeds.

Option 2 – An IRA inherited from your spouse may be rolled over into your own personal IRA account.

Option 3 – An IRA inherited by a non-spouse beneficiary must be transferred into an Inherited IRA account to manage the assets (if the IRA isn't cashed out in full).

Inherited IRAs work just like regular IRAs and have the same investment options available to them. One important difference is that rollovers into an Inherited IRA are not allowed. If moving an Inherited IRA, always make sure a direct transfer is done or else the IRS will consider the move a total distribution.

CORPORATE RETIREMENT PLAN SETUP

While individual participants may have little interest in the nuts and bolts of a corporate retirement plan setup, if you are a small business owner or on the trustee committee of a larger plan then you will need to be familiar with the inner workings of the retirement plan offered to employees. For this section we will concentrate only on plans regulated by the Department of Labor (DoL) and regulated under the Employee Retirement Income Security Act (ERISA) of 1974.

ERISA Covered Plans
401(k) Plans
403(b) Plans
Profit Sharing Plans
Employee Stock Ownership Plans (ESOPs)
Defined Benefit Plans (Pensions)

The Department of Labor has some general ERISA requirements that plan sponsors will need to follow regardless of which plan type they go with.

- A written plan that describes the benefit structure and guides day-to-day operations;

- A trust fund to hold the plan's assets

- A record keeping system to track the flow of monies going to and from the retirement plan; and

- Documents to provide plan information to employees participating in the plan and to the government.

Fiduciary Requirements

Another important aspect (and risk) of setting up a corporate retirement plan is the fiduciary requirement. The controlling parties of an ERISA regulated plan are typically required to act in a fiduciary capacity whenever handling plan assets. According to the DoL this includes:

- Acting solely in the interest of plan participants and their beneficiaries and with the exclusive purpose of providing benefits to them;

- Carrying out their duties prudently;

- Following the plan documents (unless inconsistent with ERISA);

- Diversifying plan investments; and

- Paying only reasonable plan expenses.

Plan Testing

Defined contribution plans can be a powerful tool for deferring taxes for both company employees and owners. 401(k) and profit sharing plans provide significantly higher contribution limits than individual IRAs. However, there are a number of administrative hurdles for a business to clear in order to provide a 401(k) to employees. Defined contribution plans like the 401(k) must do a test annually to insure that the plan is not discriminating in favor of a group known as "highly compensated employees" or HCEs. In 2018 a HCE is defined as:

- An owner of more than 5% of the employer in the testing year or the previous year (family stock attribution rules apply which treat an individual as owning stock owned by his spouse, children, grandchildren or parents), or

- An employee who received compensation in excess of a specified limit from the employer in the previous year (e.g., employees who earned more than $120,000 in 2017 will be considered HCEs in 2018). The employer may elect that this group be limited to the top 20% of employees based on compensation.

When performing discrimination testing not all employees must necessarily be counted. The following must be included:

- Active employees eligible for company match as of end of the year.

- An employees terminated during the year but met plan requirements for hours worked.

- All employees eligible to make after-tax contributions at any time during the year.

Plans are limited in who they may choose to exclude from plan participation. The most common exclusions are for:

- Employees under age 21.

- Employees who worked less than 1,000 hours in the last year.

- Employees covered by a union based retirement plan.

RULE OF THUMB

Retirement plan administration can be complex and burdensome. Unless you have staff highly specialized in the field of 401(k) administration your plan would be prudent to hire a third-party to help with plan administration and testing.

Actual Deferral Percentage (ADP) Test

The nondiscrimination rules require that the deferral rate of HCEs and Non-HCEs be within a certain target percentage rate. The reason for this is to prevent company owners from starting a corporate retirement plan that only benefits company owners but ignores lower paid rank and file employees.

Sample 401(k) Profit Sharing Plan ADP Test

Employee	Compensation	Deferral	ADP
HCE 1	$200,000	$12,000	6.0%
HCE 2	$150,000	$8,000	5.3%
HCE Total	**$350,000**	**$20,000**	**5.7%**
NonHCE 1	$75,000	$5,000	6.7%
NonHCE 2	$50,000	$2,500	5.0%
NonHCE 3	$40,000	$3,000	7.5%
NonHCE 4	$40,000	$0	0.0%
NonHCE 5	$25,000	$1,000	4.0%
NonHCE Total	**$230,000**	**$11,500**	**5.0%**

ADP Testing Thresholds

NonHCE %	Maximum HCE %
2% or Less	NonHCE % x 2
2%-8%	NonHCE % + 2
8% or More	NonHCE % +1.25

In the above company example the average deferral percentage for HCEs is 5.7% versus the 5.0% for NonHCEs. Because the NonHCE rate falls between 2%-8% the HCEs are allowed to contribute 2% more on average than the NonHCE ADP rate. This means the HCEs could contribute more money to the 401k until their rate reached 7.7%.

In addition to the ADP test there is the Actual Contribution Percentage (ACP) test. This test is similar to the ADP test, but it also takes into consideration employer matching contributions. Plans must pass either the ADP or ACP test or HCEs will be required to remove excess contributions.

Safe Harbor 401(k)

If the testing of your corporate plan proves troublesome there are other routes around having to satisfy the annual testing. The alternative requirement is called a Safe Harbor election and it must provide one of the following:

- A minimum 3% non-elective employee contribution or

- a 4% employee match for the first 5% of employee contributions

When investors think of defined benefit plans such as pensions, most think that these type of plans are only for big businesses or governments. However, for small businesses with the right makeup of employees, a defined benefit plan can provide a route for highly compensated employees and owners to benefit from large tax deferrals on annual contributions.

Cash Balance Plans

A popular defined benefit plan for small businesses is known as a cash balance plan. A cash balance plan is an IRS qualified plan that can provide valuable benefits to key employees. This type of plan is typically a best fit for business owners that have the following characteristics:

- 40 years old or older
- Paying a large amount of taxes with income over $250,000
- Consistent business income to support annual plan funding
- Already maximizing a 401(k) and profit sharing plan
- Looking to make high contributions in a short time frame
- Low number of full time rank and file employees

Cash balance plans can provide signficantly higher thresholds for contributions versus defined contribution plans. Particpants in these plans have the ability to save up to nearly $2 million in an account. Assuming maximum compensation ($275,000 for 2018), the following table illustrates the maximum amounts that can be reasonably credited:

Cash Balance Maximum Annual Credits	
Age	Annual Credit
40	$66,000
45	$86,000
50	$111,000
55	$144,000
60	$187,000
65	$196,000

Source: Journal of Accountancy, *Plan Design in the Balance*

SAVINGS FOR CHILDREN AND EDUCATION

Many investors desire to give money to their children as gifts or for educational needs. According to the Department of Education, in the 2013-2014 school year the average yearly cost of a 4-year public university was $18,391 and $40,917 for a private university. Once you consider the total cost of a 4-year degree plus potential post graduate work, a significant amount of funds will be needed to provide for college education. There are a number of different avenues available when saving for education needs.

Custodial Accounts

Custodial accounts are available for anyone under age 18. There are no tax benefits to funding or investing in a typical custodial account. An adult must be named custodian and, in most states, the funds revert to being under the control of the child upon reaching age 18 unless the account title provides otherwise.

The Coverdell Education IRA

A beneficiary is limited to receiving $2,000 per year in a Coverdell IRA. A beneficiary is someone who is under age 18 or is a special needs beneficiary. While there is no tax deduction for contributing to a Coverdell IRA, assets grow tax-free assuming they are distributed for qualified education expenses.

529 Plans

The most popular option for educational savings are 529 plans. Individual states sponsor plans, and investment options and tax benefits differ from state to state. Plans are split between prepaid tuition plans and college savings plans. These types of plans differ significantly.

Contribution limits to 529 plans are significantly higher than those to a Coverdell IRA. Contributions are mainly limited by current gift tax laws which limit contributions to $15,000 per year per donor to each donee in 2018. A special election may be made to front-load up to 5 years worth of contributions in one year (currently up to $75,000) free of any gift taxes. However, a gift tax return should be filed to make this election.

Qualified Expenses

Withdrawals from education accounts are federally tax-free as long as they are used for qualified higher education expenses. These expenses include:

- Tuition, fees, books, supplies, and equipment
- Reasonable costs for room and board for a student who is at least half-time
- The actual amount charged if the student is residing in educational housing

DIFFERENCES BETWEEN PREPAID AND COLLEGE SAVINGS PLANS

Prepaid Tuition Plan	College Savings Plan
Locks in tuition prices at eligible public and private colleges and universities.	No lock on college costs.
All plans cover tuition and mandatory fees only. Some plans allow you to purchase a room and board option or use excess tuition credits for other qualified expenses.	Covers all "qualified education expenses," including tuition, room & board, mandatory fees, books, computers (if required).
Most plans set lump sum and installment payments prior to purchase based on age of beneficiary and number of years of college tuition purchased.	Many plans have contribution limits in excess of $200,000.
Many state plans are guaranteed or backed by state.	No state guarantee. Most investment options are subject to market risk. Your investment may make no profit or even decline in value.
Most plans have age/grade limit for beneficiary.	No age limits. Open to adults and children.
Most state plans require either owner or beneficiary of plan to be a state resident.	No residency requirement. However, non-residents may only be able to purchase some plans through financial advisers or brokers.
Most plans have limited enrollment period.	Enrollment open all year.

Source: Smart Saving for College, FINRA

Tax benefits for contributing to a 529 plan differ from state to state. In order to obtain a tax deduction, most states require that you contribute to your resident state plan. If you are looking to contribute to a 529 plan, make sure you are not losing out on tax benefits from not investing in your home state's plan.

State	529 Tax Benefits
Alabama	$5,000 per parent ($10,000 joint)
Alaska	No state income tax
Arizona	$2,000 single or head of household/$4,000 joint (any state plan)
Arkansas	$5,000 per parent ($10,000 joint)
California	—
Colorado	Full amount of contribution
Connecticut	$5,000 per parent ($10,000 joint), 5 year carry forward on excess contributions
Delaware	—
Florida	No state income tax
Georgia	$2,000 per beneficiary
Hawaii	—
Idaho	$4,000 single/$8,000 joint
Illinois	$10,000 single/$20,000 joint per beneficiary (25% tax credit for employers for matching contributions up to $500 per employee)
Indiana	20% tax credit on contributions up to $5,000 ($1,000 maximum credit)
Iowa	$3,163 single/$6,326 joint per account
Kansas	$3,000 single/$6,000 joint per beneficiary (any state plan), above the line exclusion from income
Kentucky	—
Louisiana	$2,400 single/$4,800 joint per beneficiary, above the line exclusion from income, unlimited carry forward of unused deduction into subsequent years
Maine	$250 per beneficiary starting 2007 (any state plan), above the line exclusion from income, phase-out at $100,000 single/$200,000 joint
Maryland	$2,500 per account per beneficiary, 10 year carry forward
Massachusetts	—
Michigan	$5,000 single/$10,000 joint, above the line exclusion from income

State	529 Tax Benefits
Minnesota	—
Mississippi	$10,000 single/$20,000 joint, above the line exclusion from income
Missouri	$8,000 single/$16,000 joint, above the line exclusion from income
Montana	$3,000 single/$6,000 joint, above the line exclusion from income
Nebraska	$10,000 per tax return ($5,000 if filing separate), above the line exclusion from income
Nevada	No state income tax
New Hampshire	—
New Jersey	—
New Mexico	Full amount of contribution, above the line exclusion from income
New York	$5,000 single/$10,000 joint, above the line exclusion from income
North Carolina	—
North Dakota	$5,000 single/$10,000 joint
Ohio	$2,000 per beneficiary per contributor or married couple, above the line exclusion from income, unlimited carry forward of excess contributions
Oklahoma	$10,000 single/$20,000 joint per beneficiary, above the line exclusion from income, five year carry forward of excess contributions
Oregon	$2,265 single/$4,530 joint (i.e., $2,265 per contributor) per year, above the line exclusion from income, four year carry forward of excess contributions
Pennsylvania	$14,000 per contributor/$28,000 joint per beneficiary (any state plan)
Rhode Island	$500 single/$1,000 joint, above the line exclusion from income, unlimited carry forward of excess contributions
South Carolina	Full amount of contribution, above the line exclusion from income
South Dakota	No state income tax
Tennessee	—
Texas	No state income tax
Utah	5% tax credit on contributions of up to $1,900 single/$3,800 joint per beneficiary (credit of $95 single/$190 joint)
Vermont	10% tax credit on up to $2,500 in contributions per beneficiary (up to $250 tax credit per taxpayer per beneficiary)
Virginia	$4,000 per account per year (no limit age 70 and older), above the line exclusion from income, unlimited carry forward of excess contributions

State	529 Tax Benefits
Washington, DC	$4,000 single/$8,000 joint, above the line exclusion from income
Washington	No state income tax
West Virginia	Full amount of contribution up to extent of income, above the line exclusion from income, five-year carry forward of excess contributions
Wisconsin	$3,000 per dependent beneficiary, self or grandchild, above the line exclusion from income
Wyoming	No state income tax

Source: www.finaid.org 2017

CHAPTER 7:

DISTRIBUTION

PREPARING FOR RETIREMENT

A Comprehensive Guide to Financial Planning

DISTRIBUTION

After decades of accumulating assets, it will eventually become time to start distributing these assets once you enter retirement. Equal effort should be put toward building a successful distribution model compared to the effort exerted in saving for retirement. A poorly built distribution strategy can derail years of retirement savings.

When designing an income strategy, it's important to consider two things: the total amount of income needed to meet your retirement needs and the relative safety of income sources that are available. You must look at your "guaranteed" income sources and figure out if there is a monthly shortfall that must be met from "non-guaranteed" sources such as investment income or savings draw-downs.

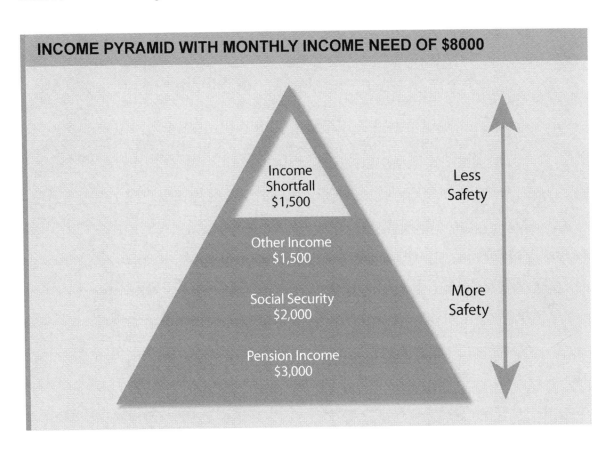

INCOME PYRAMID WITH MONTHLY INCOME NEED OF $8000

Income Shortfall $1,500

Other Income $1,500

Social Security $2,000

Pension Income $3,000

Less Safety

More Safety

Static and Dynamic Spending Needs

Another way to look at your expenses is determining whether your specific spending needs qualify as being "static" or "dynamic" in nature. A static spending need does not change on a monthly or annual basis; such a need might be your mortgage or car insurance payments. In income planning, it can be helpful to pair static expenses with static income sources (guaranteed income sources like social security or a pension).

Dynamic expenses are more variable in nature. Discretionary expenses such as a vacation or a new car are subject to more flexibility than a static expense. To fund dynamic expenses you may want to utilize dynamic income sources like an investment account that will have a value that varies on an annual basis.

Pensions are relatively simple from both an accumulation and distribution standpoint with regard to retirement saving. For most defined benefit plans, the longer you hold off taking benefits, the greater your benefits will be.

The main decision you'll have to make with regard to a pension is deciding on whether you want your spouse covered upon your death. A typical selection you'll be given looks like this:

Single	50% to Survivor	100% to Survivor
$3,000	$2,500	$2,000

Lump Sum Benefits

Some pension plans allow the option to take a lump sum payment instead of a monthly benefit. In exchange for forgoing a monthly benefit, a lump sum payment will instead cash out your entire pension balance in one single payment. This payment can then be rolled into an IRA without taxes. The employee can then manage income needs (instead of the employer).

The main advantage of a lump sum payment is the control it provides the retiree. Instead of payments being dictated by your pension plan, the retiree can control the timing and amounts of distributions (subject to required minimum distribution rules). Of course, with this advantage comes the responsibility of not overspending and depleting your funds early in retirement.

Pension Maximization

Many couples simply choose the 100% joint pension benefit option that covers both spouses. However, there is a technique to potentially maximize future benefits and take more control of your benefits through the usage of life insurance.

Consider a married 62 year-old retiree with the following monthly benefit options available:

Single	50% to Survivor	100% to Survivor
$3,000	$2,500	$2,000

There is a $1000 per month difference between the full single life payout and full joint benefit. The retiree could elect for the higher $3,000/month payment and then take the extra $1000 in income to purchase a permanent life insurance policy. For a healthy 62 year-old, this could potentially buy close to $500,000 in coverage.

In this scenario, if the spouse were to predecease the covered retiree, then the retiree would have the option to cancel the life insurance policy and continue taking the larger single life payout.

Note: If you are an unmarried couple or have a non-traditional marriage that is not recognized by the state, you may be unable to select a joint pension benefit option. In these situations a pension maximization strategy may be the only way to effectively cover the financial interests of both parties.

However, if the covered retiree dies first, then the spouse will receive $500,000 in a lump sum life insurance settlement. With a 4% withdrawal rate, this sum of money can provide a $2,000 benefit to the spouse—the same amount that was expected under the 100% to survivor option.

Pension maximization doesn't work for all scenarios and should be considered carefully. Pension maximization is most beneficial when:

- The retiree is in good health (lower life insurance premiums)
- There is a large difference between single and joint pension payouts
- The retiring spouse is significantly younger (longer life expectancy)

Should you select single life on a pension payout and die early in retirement, your beneficiary isn't completely out of luck. Most pensions plans have a "pension balance" that if it hasn't already been paid out prior to the retiree's death will be distributed as a lump sum to a beneficiary.

RULE OF THUMB

Never make a pension election based on a pension maximization strategy until you've been underwritten for insurance. There is never a guarantee that you'll be able to get the insurance you need.

Pension Benefit Guarantee Corporation (PBGC)

While pensions are easy for employees to participate in and understand, they are not nearly as simple for sponsors to operate. Because of this, it is possible for a pension to "go bust" due to not being able to afford promised payments to current and future retirees.

What happens to your pension's benefits should your plan provider default? Most private pensions are required to fund the Pension Benefit Guarantee Corporation (PBGC), which is an independent agency of the United States government that was created by the Employee Retirement Income Security Act of 1974 (ERISA).

In exchange for these insurance payments, a pension is guaranteed a certain percentage of benefits to participants. While participants may not receive their full benefit, there is a percentage that will be guaranteed.

In 2017, PBGC insurance benefits capped at $5,369.32 per month for a worker who was 65.

PBGC only covers private pensions. It provides no coverage for public, state and local municipalities. Failures by these pensions are typically covered under state law and have been less frequent than private failures. However, with many state pension plans being significantly underfunded, this could grow into a greater issue in years and decades to come. Several states are under a 30% funding threshold whereas a healthy corporation typically exceeds 85%.

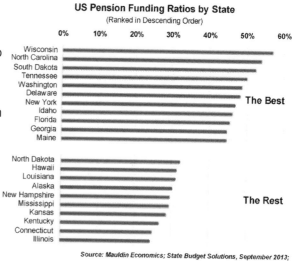

US Pension Funding Ratios by State
(Ranked in Descending Order)

Source: Mauldin Economics; State Budget Solutions, September 2013;
Manhattan Institute for Policy Research, August 2013

Defined Contribution Plans

With defined contribution plans such as a 401(k), 403(b), or 457, the plan participant is in total control of distributions. As early as age 55, participants have the option to begin penalty-free withdrawals (age 59½ for IRAs). Keep in mind that any withdrawals from these accounts will be subject to income taxation (except for Roth distributions). While total control can be a nice benefit, it does present the challenge of creating a viable distribution strategy for your assets.

INVESTMENT DEVICES AND STRATEGIES FOR RETIREMENT INCOME

– Bond ladders

– Dividend paying stocks/funds

– Straight annuities

– Annuity riders

Bond Ladders

Through the use of bonds (or any other type of fixed income investment), it is possible to build a reliable income stream through a laddering strategy. By selecting multiple fixed income securities, it's possible to custom build a bond ladder with the desired maturity and yield characteristics that you are looking for in your portfolio. Since each individual bond will pay interest on a different date, it is possible to have bond interest continually flowing out of a portfolio that can then be used for retirement income purposes.

SAMPLE BOND LADDER	
20 Year Corporate Bond	7% Yield
15 Year Corporate Bond	6% Yield
10 Year Corporate Bond	4% Yield
5 Year US Treasury Bond	1% Yield
Total Average Yield 4.5% Yield	
Total Average Maturity 12.5 Years	

RULE OF THUMB

It is best to have $50,000 or more in order to properly construct a diversified bond ladder. Many bonds have purchase minimums of $5,000, so if you have a smaller portfolio, it's best to stick to mutual funds and ETFs for bond investing.

Dividends

Dividend paying stocks and mutual funds can be used to create an income stream the same way a bond ladder works. However, investors must remember that dividends are paid out by stocks that tend be more volatile in nature than fixed income. While using dividend paying stocks is a fully viable way to create income in retirement, such a strategy does bear greater risk than a bond ladder. Just keep in mind that your portfolio value and income stream will be subject to greater volatility.

Straight Annuities

It is possible give a portion (or all) of your qualified assets to an insurance company in return for a straight annuity. In return for your up front premiums, an insurance company will agree to pay you a set amount of money for the rest or your life, just like a pension. If you don't like the idea of being in control of managing your retirement income, a straight annuity might be a viable solution.

THE MORE THESE 3 VARIABLES INCREASE THE MORE THE PAYOUT OF A STRAIGHT ANNUITY WILL RISE:

– Your age

– Amount invested in annuity

– Current interest rate environment

Straight annuities can be constructed in two ways: (1) You can take an **immediate straight annuity** after which the insurance company will begin an immediate payout; (2) You select a **deferred straight annuity** for which the insurance company will agree to begin payments at a set date later in time. Many times insurance companies will allow fixed, variable, and indexed annuities to be "annuitized" meaning that their value is converted into a straight annuity.

Fixed Annuities

Similar in function to a bank CD, fixed annuities provide a guaranteed rate of return to investors for a set period of time.

Variable Annuities

Variable annuities are similar to mutual funds as they typically do not guarantee a rate or return or a return of principal. Investment accounts in these contracts are referred to as sub-accounts and can provide a wide array of investment choices.

Indexed Annuities

Indexed annuities meld many of the characteristics of fixed and variable annuities together. Typically these contracts have a guaranteed return of capital similar to a fixed annuity, but can also provide a variable rate of return based on market indexes similar to a variable annuity.

Annuity Income Riders

Income riders have grown more and more popular on variable and indexed annuities over the past decade. At their core, income riders act like a deferred straight annuity. In order to understand income riders, it's important to understand the different values of an annuity function.

A good way to look at an annuity is to separate out the different values you'll see on your account into different buckets. The amount in each bucket is independent of the other buckets.

Contract Value

The contract value is the actual value of your contract. If your contract has no surrender fee then this is the amount a contract could be liquidated for today.

Death Benefit

A death benefit is the minimum amount your beneficiary is guaranteed to inherit at your death. Typically the death benefit is guaranteed to never decrease even if the underlying contract decreases in value.

Withdrawal Benefit Base

This is the base of which a contract can be annuitized. On a typical income rider, the withdrawal benefit base will be guaranteed to increase between 5% and 8% annually. It's important to remember that this guaranteed increase is on the withdrawal benefit base only, not the underlying contract value.

Withdrawal Benefit

This is the income amount a contract is guaranteed to pay out for the entire life of the annuitant. Once the withdrawal benefit is turned on, it will decrease the contract value by the same distribution amount each year. Should the contract value decrease to zero, the withdrawal benefit is still guaranteed to pay out for life. The advantage of a withdrawal benefit is that it guarantees you won't outlive the income being generated from your investment.

Income Rider Costs

There are obvious advantages to using income riders on an annuity contract. However, these benefits aren't offered for free from the insurance companies. Typical income riders cost between 1-2%, which can take the total internal fees within an annuity to over 4%. With such a high fee hurdle to clear, it can become hard to increase the contract value if such a rider is elected.

Annuity Income Rider Example

This example demonstrates a 65 year old who places $100,000 into an annuity contract that earns 3% annually and has a 7% annual increase to the withdrawal benefit base. At age 80, the withdrawal benefit is activated, and it pays 5% of the withdrawal benefit base annually until age 95.

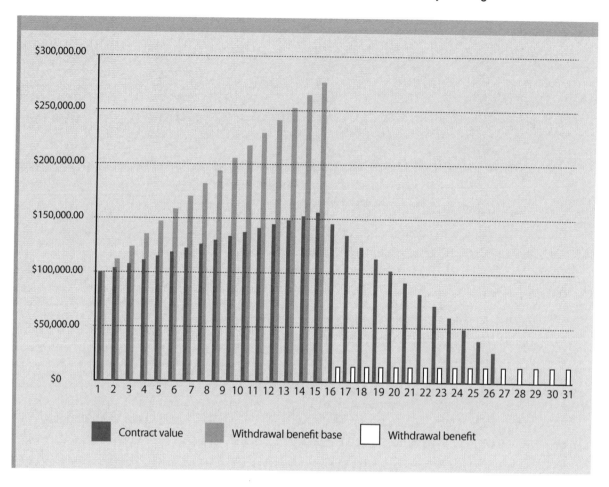

Initial Contract Value	$100,000
Contract Value at Age 80	$155,796.74
Withdrawal Benefit Base at Age 80	$275,903.15
Withdrawal Benefit at Age 80	$13,795.16
Total Benefits Paid at Age 95	$220,722.52
30 Year Rate of Return on Income Rider:	**3.64%**

While the withdrawal benefit base in this scenario is guaranteed to grow at 7%, the real rate of return realized from this benefit was only 3.64%. While the guaranteed income can be a useful tool in retirement planning, the rate of return realized from withdrawal benefits is fairly low.

Required Minimum Distributions (RMDs)

In some cases you may not need nor want to take (and be taxed on) a distribution from your 401(k) or IRA. While you might be okay not taking a distribution, the IRS is not. Upon reaching age 70 ½, everyone is required to take a required minimum distribution from their tax-deferred retirement vehicles. This ensures that the IRS collects regular tax revenue from these tax-deferred vehicles.

IRS Required Minimum Distribution Table

In order to calculate your RMD, you must look up the distribution period for your age within the IRS Uniform Lifetime table. You then divide your total qualified assets by your distribution period.

Retiree Age	Distribution Period	Retiree Age	Distribution Period	Retiree Age	Distribution Period
70	27.4	86	14.1	102	5.5
71	26.5	87	13.4	103	5.2
72	25.6	88	12.7	104	4.9
73	24.7	89	12	105	4.5
74	23.8	90	11.4	106	4.2
75	22.9	91	10.8	107	3.9
76	22	92	10.2	108	3.7
77	21.2	93	9.6	109	3.4
78	20.3	94	9.1	110	3.1
79	19.5	95	8.6	111	2.9
80	18.7	96	8.1	112	2.6
81	17.9	97	7.6	113	2.4
82	17.1	98	7.1	114	2.1
83	16.3	99	6.7	115	1.9
84	15.5	100	6.3	116	1.9
85	14.8	101	5.9	117	1.9

RMD EXAMPLE FOR 75 YEAR OLD

Account	Value
IRA #1	$50,000
IRA #2	$50,000
401(k)	$150,000
Totals	$250,000

$250,000 / 22.9 = $10,917.03

$10,917.03 can be taken from one account or split between multiple accounts.

RMDs Upon Age 70 ½

Upon reaching age 70 ½, you will be required to take an RMD, but you will have the choice to take it either the year you turn 70 ½ or the following year by April 1st. Should you wait to take it in the following year, you will be required to take your age 70 ½ RMD and your age 71 RMD in the same year. While this strategy allows you to defer the receipt of income, the receipt of two RMDs could potentially push you into a higher income tax bracket in the year in which they are received.

Mandatory withdrawals are not required from a Roth IRA. However, you must take annual RMDs from traditional, SEP and SIMPLE IRAs, pension and profit-sharing plans and 401(k), 403(b), and 457 retirement plans. Severe financial penalties of 50% of your RMD amount will be assessed for non-compliance with the rule.

If you are still working as an employee at age 70 ½, you aren't required to take RMDs from an employer's sponsored 401(k), 403(b), 457 plan, profit-sharing plan, or pension plan. Your initial RMDs from these accounts will be required only after you terminate your employment. However, RMDs are required from these types of accounts if you own 5% or more of a business sponsoring such a retirement plan. You must take RMDs from IRAs after you turn 70 ½ regardless of your employment status.

RMDs from an Inherited IRA

When you inherit an IRA, you may be required to take required minimum distributions. The options available will depend on your relationship to the deceased from whom you have inherited the IRA.

If a spouse is named as the primary beneficiary of an IRA, that person has the following options after the holder's death:

- Lump-sum distribution

- Establish a beneficiary IRA account and eventually begin RMDs

- Deplete the entire balance before the end of the fifth year following the year of the IRA holder's death (available if the IRA holder had not started RMDs, i.e., died before age 70½, or the inherited IRA is a Roth IRA)

- Roll the assets into spouse's IRA (and name own beneficiaries)

A non-spouse beneficiary has all the same options as above except for the last option of rolling the assets into that person's own IRA.

RMDs as a Withdrawal Strategy

Do required minimum distributions make a viable withdrawal strategy? According to a 2012 study on withdrawal rates by the Center for Retirement Research at Boston College, the answer may be yes. Based on their findings, simply taking RMDs, as indicated by the IRS tables, may actually be a more efficient distribution strategy than taking a fixed 4% withdrawal or simply taking distributions of dividends/interest. Of course, this strategy is only viable for those with significant amounts saved in tax-deferred retirement accounts.

Early Withdrawals with 72(t)

Generally, there is a 10% penalty assessed if an individual takes a distribution from a qualified account before reaching age 59 ½. This can make early retirement more difficult for individuals needing to access qualified funds. However, the IRS does have one provision for individuals in this situation. Internal Revenue code section 72(t) provides for a Series of Substantial Equal Payments (SOSEP). This provision may allow access to qualified funds as early as age 55 by taking annual distributions.

"Stretch" IRA

The term "stretch" IRA is one that has been popularized over the past decade. In its simplest form, a stretch IRA extends qualified assets as long as possible for a family across generations. Qualified assets can be stretched by naming younger beneficiaries for these assets. Because of their younger age, RMDs will also be smaller, thus making their assets "stretch" longer.

Net Unrealized Appreciation (NUA)

A unique distribution strategy is available to those who have appreciated employer stock within their 401(k). The employer stock can be distributed from the 401(k), and income tax is only due on the cost basis of stock. Should the stock be sold after distribution, then capital gains taxes would be due on the appreciation. If there is a significant difference between the marginal income tax rate and capital gains tax rates, then NUA gives greater tax savings. Consider the following example:

	Rollover Option	NUA Option
Total Market Value	$500,000	$500,000
Taxes Due On Rollover	$0	$33,000 (33% Marginal Rate on $100,000 income)
Taxes Due on Liquidation	$175,000 (35% Marginal Rate)	$60,000 (LTCG Rate of 15% on $400,000 Capital Gains)
Total Tax Paid	$175,000	$93,000
Tax Savings	–	$82,000

Employer stock with $100,000 cost basis and 35% marginal tax bracket

Social Security

Social Security was passed into law in 1935 by the Roosevelt administration, and today it provides vital income for over 58 million Americans. In 2017, the average benefits paid to all retired workers was $1,369 receiving benefits. This is a replacement income ratio of around 40% for the average worker.

While its primary design was to provide retirement income, Social Security includes the following four categories:

- Retirement   – Disability

- Dependents   – Survivor benefits

Eligibility

To become eligible for Social Security, you must earn 40 credits to qualify on your own accord. A credit is 3 months of employment. To earn 4 credits for 2018, you needed to earn $5,280 in covered earnings. If you qualify for Social Security, you also qualify for Medicare at age 65.

In years past, the Social Security Administration mailed out annual earning and payment statements to workers. These estimate statements have been suspended. To inquire about your benefits, you will now need to visit a local Social Security office or visit their website at www.ssa.gov. These estimates will show your expected benefits at full retirement age (FRA) and early retirement (age 62). Additionally, the estimates are based on your 35 years of highest income and assume you will continue working until the year you elect benefits.

RULE OF THUMB

Apply for Social Security benefits 3 months prior to the date you wish to receive benefits. The application process is not instantaneous.

Social Security Full Retirement Age (FRA) and Early Reductions

The full retirement age is trending upward for those born between 1938 and 1959.
This change in full retirement age was passed in 1984 by the Reagan administration and has taken decades to implement.

Date of Birth	Full Retirement Age	Reduction at 62
Before 1938	65	20%
1938	65 & 2 Months	20.83%
1939	65 & 4 Months	21.67%
1940	65 & 6 Months	22.50%
1941	65 & 8 Months	23.33%
1942	65 & 10 Months	24.17%
1943-1954	66	25%
1955	66 & 2 Months	25.83%
1956	66 & 4 Months	26.67%
1957	66 & 6 Months	27.50%
1958	66 & 8 Months	28.33%
1959	66 & 10 Months	29.17%
After 1959	67	30%

The earliest you can elect to take retirement benefits from Social Security is age 62. Social Security retirement benefits continue to accumulate on a monthly basis until age 70. Benefits cease to increase at age 70 even if a worker delays taking benefits.

Year of Birth	Yearly Rate of Increase	Monthly Rate of Increase
1933-1934	5.5%	0.46%
1935-1936	6.0%	0.50%
1937-1938	6.5%	0.54%
1939-1940	7.0%	0.58%
1941-1942	7.5%	0.63%
1943 or later	8.0%	0.67%

Break Even Analysis Between Early Benefits (62) and Full Retirement Age (66)

Age	Benefits at 62	Total	Benefits at 66	Total	Difference
62	$18,000.00	$18,000.00	–	–	$18,000.00
63	$18,000.00	$36,000.00	–	–	$36,000.00
64	$18,000.00	$54,000.00	–	–	$54,000.00
65	$18,000.00	$72,000.00	–	–	$72,000.00
66	$18,000.00	$90,000.00	$ 24,000.00	$ 24,000.00	$66,000.00
67	$18,000.00	$08,000.00	$24,000.00	$48,000.00	$ 60,000.00
68	$18,000.00	$126,000.00	$24,000.00	$72,000.00	$ 54,000.00
69	$18,000.00	$144,000.00	$24,000.00	$96,000.00	$48,000.00
70	$18,000.00	$162,000.00	$24,000.00	$120,000.00	$42,000.00
71	$18,000.00	$180,000.00	$24,000.00	$144,000.00	$36,000.00
72	$18,000.00	$198,000.00	$24,000.00	$168,000.00	$30,000.00
73	$18,000.00	$216,000.00	$24,000.00	$192,000.00	$24,000.00
74	$18,000.00	$234,000.00	$24,000.00	$216,000.00	$18,000.00
75	$18,000.00	$252,000.00	$24,000.00	$240,000.00	$12,000.00
76	$18,000.00	$270,000.00	$24,000.00	$264,000.00	$6,000.00
77	$18,000.00	$288,000.00	$24,000.00	$288,000.00	$ -
78	$18,000.00	$306,000.00	$24,000.00	$312,000.00	$ (6,000.00)

The break-even age for someone electing early benefits in this scenario is age 77. The individual in this example receives more benefits over time if he delays taking benefits until full retirement age and lives past age 77. This data assumes no investment of Social Security benefits. If benefits are invested the break-even age extends further.

Break-Even Age If Social Security Benefits Are Invested

Rate of Return	Break Even Age
1%	78
2%	79
3%	81
4%	83
5%	86
6%	92
7%	109
7.5% or Greater	Never

Based on investing early benefits at age 62 versus FRA benefits at age 66.

It is possible to elect early Social Security payments while you continue to work. However, if you elect to do so, you will have a reduction in benefits should your earned income surpass certain thresholds. Only earned income counts in this calculation, and earned income of a spouse is not considered in the calculation.

Age	Benefit Reduction	Per Income	2018 Annual Income Limit
Age 62 to end of year prior to FRA	$1	$2	$17,040
In the year you reach FRA	$1	$3	$45,360
Starting with the month you reach FRA	$0	-	No Earnings Limit

BENEFIT REDUCTION EXAMPLE

– A worker retires at age 62 and elects benefits of $18,000 annually.

– At age 63 he decides to go back to work making $20,000 per year.

($20,000 - $17,040) ÷ 2 = $1,480 Benefit Reduction

Social Security payments will be reduced by $1,480 in this scenario because the worker made $2,960 more than the $17,040 annual income limit. While this benefit is lost for the year, it is not totally forfeited. The reduced benefit amount will go back toward benefit accumulation for subsequent years.

Taxation of Social Security Benefits

As part of the Reagan administration Social Security overhaul of 1984, Social Security benefits are now potentially subject to income taxation. A panel headed by Alan Greenspan made this recommendation.

% of Benefits Taxable	Single Filer	Married Filer
0%	Below $25,000	Below $32,000
Up to 50%	$25,000 - $34,000	$32,000 - $44,000
Up to 85%	Greater than $34,000	Greater than $44,000

Windfall Benefit Provisions

You could have a further reduction to your Social Security payments if you are a state or government employee. The Windfall Elimination Provision (WEP) may reduce Social Security benefits for those workers who earned a pension but did not withhold Social Security taxes from earned wages.

The reason for this provision is that Social Security benefit calculations are weighted to pay a higher percentage to workers with lower Social Security-covered career earnings. The WEP removes this advantage so that these workers won't receive a large pension and full Social Security benefits when they had no Social Security withholdings.

Spousal Benefits

A spouse is eligible to receive the higher of the following upon reaching full retirement age:

1. Their own earned Social Security benefit.

2. Half of their spouse's benefit.

There is an additional reduction should spousal benefits be elected prior to full retirement age.

Spouse's Age	% of Retirees Benefit
62	35%
63	37.5%
64	42%
65	46%
66	50%

Spouses looking to maximize Social Security benefits have the following strategies available:

File & Suspend

A spousal benefit can be taken only if your working spouse has filed for social security benefits. If the working spouse has no intentions of retiring, then he can file for Social Security benefits and suspend receiving any payments. This will have no negative effects on the working spouse's future benefit, but will allow for the spousal election to begin.

Do-Over

In the past, it was possible to take early retirement benefits and then repay them to the Social Security Administration interest-free and begin a higher benefit. This strategy has been limited now, and the time frame to repay benefits is limited to 12 months after first taking benefits.

Death Benefits

Upon the death of a spouse, the surviving spouse receives the following:

- A step-up in benefits to the same amount of their deceased spouse if the deceased spouse was the higher earner.
- Reduced benefits as early as age 60 (don't have to wait until age 62).
- A $255 one-time lump sum death benefit.

Divorce Benefits

It's possible to receive a spousal benefit even if you are divorced. You'll need to meet the following requirements to qualify:

- Married for at least 10 years

- Former spouse is eligible for benefits

- Are at least 62 years old

- Remain unmarried

A spousal benefit can be collected 2 years after a divorce even if the ex-spouse has not begun collecting benefits. The spousal benefit will have no effect on the benefit of the ex-spouse.

Other Sources of Retirement Income

Life Insurance can be a viable source of retirement income in your financial planning. The death benefit can be used to replace lost income from the deceased spouse. Additionally, with permanent policies there could be large sums of cash value accumulated which can be taken to provide retirement income.

Reverse Mortgages are usually used as a last resort in retirement income planning. A reverse mortgage involves taking the equity out of your home in the opposite way of which a mortgage typically works. It is up to beneficiaries to pay off this mortgage upon the debtor's death, and should the mortgage not be satisfied, the property is kept by the mortgage holder.

Inheritances can be a significant source of retirement income, but it is extremely dangerous to rely solely on such a windfall. There is no guarantee that you will be named a beneficiary, and it is also possible that the assets you are counting on will be spent down during the life of the current owner(s).

CHAPTER 8:

RISK MANAGEMENT

PREPARING FOR RETIREMENT

A COMPREHENSIVE GUIDE TO FINANCIAL PLANNING

RISK MANAGEMENT

After a lifetime of saving and accumulating assets, many people enjoy their greatest net worth just prior to retirement. To suffer a large financial loss at this time could be devastating to the success of your retirement plan. Imagine suffering a debilitating car accident in the years leading up to retirement. It's possible you could be without wages for years, and if the accident was your fault, you could be liable for thousands of dollars in damages as well.

Insurance transfers economic risk from a policy holder to the insurance company. With respect to financial and retirement planning, most of the major risks that could derail your retirement are able to be alleviated through the proper use of insurance. A comprehensive insurance review is highly advisable for a pre-retiree (and younger adults as well).

This chapter will focus on identifying and managing risk through the use of insurance:

- Disability income insurance
- Medicare / Medicaid
- Liability insurance
- Health insurance
- Long-term care insurance
- Life insurance – term and cash value

Disability Income Insurance

Most people take for granted one of their largest financial assets: themselves. The value of your ability to earn income should not be underestimated. According to standard mortality tables, a working adult is at least twice as likely to suffer disability versus death during their career. However, many people overlook this risk, which can be devastating to a well-constructed retirement plan.

Disability insurance is designed to replace a portion of your income, not the entire amount. The partial replacement incentivizes an injured worker to return to work. Most insurance companies will not provide coverage for more than 60% of your current wage base.

- **Short–term disability insurance** generally lasts several months or up to a year and will pay out in weekly benefits. It can be more cost effective to "self-insure" against short-term disability by maintaining adequate liquidity.

- **Long–term disability insurance** pays after an elimination period. Policies can have elimination periods between 30 days and 1 year. Shorter elimination periods increase the cost of a policy. The benefit period varies by policy, but can last until age 65. The potential income loss from a long-term disability makes it difficult for one to self-insure against such a disability.

When shopping for long-term disability insurance, you must consider how difficult your job would be after sustaining a significant injury. If you work a desk job, you may be able to return to work if you were disabled and in a wheel chair. However, if you move pianos for a living, it's unlikely you could return to your job. For this reason, it's important to choose a policy that is appropriate for your own occupation.

Other Disability Income Sources

– Social Security disability requires that you cannot work at any occupation for which you are qualified. This may be challenging to prove. In addition, the disability must have lasted or be expected to last 12 months or to result in death.

– Workers' compensation may be available if the injury and disability were work related. Benefits (usually 2/3 of wages) are free from income taxation.

Health Insurance

Regardless of age, obtaining proper health insurance coverage is critical to a sound financial plan. There are a number of ways health insurance can be obtained:

– Employer Group Policy	– COBRA
– Individual Policy	– Insurance Exchanges
– Medicare	– Medicaid

Medicare eligibility begins at age 65. If your goal is to retire prior to age 65, you must plan to bridge the gap to Medicare coverage. If you are providing insurance coverage for a younger spouse, remember they'll need to be 65 as well to qualify for Medicare. Identifying adequate and affordable coverage during this time period may be the difference in being able to retire early.

The Consolidated Omnibus Budget Reconciliation Act of 1985 (COBRA) can typically only be utilized for up to 18 or 36 months and can have a hefty price tag. It will usually cost the full unsubsidized premium of the insurance. Individual policies are something else to consider, but make sure you qualify for coverage *before* leaving the work place. With health care costs continuing to increase, expect policies to have higher deductibles in the future.

Health insurance exchanges went live in 2013 as part of the Patient Protection and Affordable Care Act of 2010. While these exchanges are relatively new, it is the intent of these exchanges to offer policies that are guaranteed issued and will have no lifetime or annual limitations.

Affordable Care Act (ACA)

Many portions of the Affordable Care Act (commonly referred to as "Obamacare") went into place in late 2013 amidst an extremely contentious setting in Congress. Given the nature and scope of the law it inevitably will change significantly in years to come.

Under the ACA, the majority of individuals were required to obtain health insurance that covers ten "essential" benefits that include ambulatory patient care, emergency services, hospitalization, maternity/newborn care, mental health and substance abuse disorder services, prescription drugs, rehabilitative and habilitative services, laboratory services, preventive services, and pediatric services. Individuals that did not elect coverage were subject to a penalty/tax. The 2017 Tax Cut and Jobs Act repealed the ACA penalty going forward.

To assist the mandate the federal government created www.healthcare.gov which acts as an insurance exchange that allows insurance companies to offer coverage across state lines. Additionally, an individual may also receive a tax subsidy for purchasing coverage depending on income levels. These subsidies are only available for those who are self-employed, unemployed, or work for a company that does not offer affordable, comprehensive insurance. "Affordable" is defined as individual coverage that costs less than 9.5% of income.

The lower one's income, the greater the subsidy. Insurance subsidies are based one's Modified Adjusted Gross Income (MAGI) in relation to the federal poverty line. The 2017 income thresholds show who would potentially be eligible for a subsidy. Subsidies are not wealth based, so you can have an unlimited amount of assets and qualify for assistance if your income level qualifies.

Household Size	Percent of Federal Poverty Line 2017					
	100%	133%	150%	200%	300%	400%
1	$12,600	$16,758	$18,900	$25,200	$37,800	$50,400
2	$16,240	$21,599	$24,360	$32,480	$48,720	$64,960
3	$20,420	$27,159	$30,630	$40,840	$61,260	$81,680
4	$24,600	$32,718	$36,900	$49,200	$73,800	$98,400
5	$28,780	$38,277	$43,170	$57,560	$86,340	$115,120
6	$32,960	$43,837	$49,440	$65,920	$98,880	$131,840
Each Additional Add	$4,180	$5,559	$6,270	$8,360	$12,540	$16,720

Note: To find out specific tax subsidies one must use a subsidy calculator which are available online.

Medicare

Medicare is a social insurance program administered by the United States government, providing health insurance coverage to people who are age 65 and over, or who meet other specific criteria.

The Social Security Amendments of 1965 were signed into law by President Lyndon Johnson. Johnson enrolled former President Harry S. Truman as the first Medicare beneficiary and presented him with the first Medicare card. Medicare now provides health care for over 40 million individuals.

MEDICARE IS DIVIDED INTO FOUR PARTS:

Part A: Hospital Insurance

Part B: Medical Insurance

Part C: Medicare Advantage Plans

Part D: Comprehensive Prescription Drug Coverage

MEDICARE PART A: HOSPITAL INSURANCE COVERAGE

No Premium Costs if Eligible for Social Security

Inpatient Hospital Care

Limited Stays at Skilled Nursing Facilities

Hospice Care

MEDICARE PART B: MEDICAL INSURANCE COVERAGE

$134/month Premium for Enrollment (Increases for Higher Incomes)

Premiums Deducted from Social Security

Pays for Doctor's Fees

Ambulance Services

Vaccinations

Mobility Equipment

X-rays and Other Diagnostics

Medicare Part B Cost

The majority of the population pays the Medicare Part B standard premium amount. However, higher income earners may pay an Income Related Monthly Adjustment Amount (IRMAA). Medicare uses the modified adjusted gross income (MAGI) reported on your IRS tax return from 2 years ago (the most recent tax return information provided to Social Security by the IRS).

Medicare Part B Cost Income Thresholds			
Single Income	**Joint Income**	**Married Filing Separately Income**	**Monthly Part B Premium**
$85,000 or less	$170,000 or less	$85,000 or less	$134.00
$85,001-$107,000	$170,001-$214,000	Not applicable	$187.50
$107,001-$133,500	$214,001-$267,000	Not applicable	$267.90
$133,501-$160,000	$267,001-$320,000	Not applicable	$348.30
$160,000 or more	$320,001 or more	Above $85,000	$428.60

Note: If you don't sign up for Part B when first eligible you may have to pay a late enrollment fee when you do eventually sign up.

Medicare Part C: Medicare Advantage Plans

With passage of the Balanced Budget Act of 1997, Medicare beneficiaries were given the option to receive their Medicare benefits through private health insurance plans instead of through the original Medicare plan (Parts A and B). These programs are known as "Medicare Choice" or "Part C" plans.

For people who choose to enroll in a Medicare Advantage health plan, Medicare pays the private health plan a fixed amount every month. Members typically pay a monthly premium in addition to the Medicare Part B premium to cover items not covered by traditional Medicare (Parts A & B), such as prescription drugs, dental care, vision care, and gym or health club memberships. In exchange for these extra benefits, enrollees may be limited in the providers through which they can receive services without paying extra.

Medicare Advantage plans are required to offer coverage that meets or exceeds the standards set by the original Medicare program, but they do not have to cover every benefit in the same way. Medicare Part C premiums will depend on the plan you select.

Medicare Part D: Prescription Drug Plans

Part D is designed to subsidize the costs of prescription drugs for Medicare beneficiaries. Anyone receiving Part A or Part B is eligible for Part D. As with Medicare Part C, coverage is not standardized.

Most Medicare beneficiaries must affirmatively enroll in a Part D plan to participate. Annual enrollment periods typically last from November 15 to December 31 of the previous plan year. Medicare beneficiaries who were eligible but did not enroll during the enrollment period must pay a late-enrollment penalty to receive Part D benefits. This penalty is equal to 1% of the national average premium times the number of full calendar months that they were eligible but not enrolled in Part D. The penalty raises the premium of Part D for beneficiaries, when and if they elect coverage.

Medicaid

Medicaid is a form of welfare and is the federally and state jointly operated health insurance program for individuals with low income and resources. It is the largest source of funding for medical and health-related services for people with limited income in the United States. As of 2014, one can qualify for Medicaid under expanded provisions if their income is 133% or less of the poverty line. Consider the following 2017 Medicaid statistics from www.medicaid.gov:

Covers over 75 million Americans, or 1 in 4 individuals

Provides medical coverage for estimated 40% of child births

Accounts for over half of Long Term Care Spending

Accounts for 17% of all Health Care Expenditures

Long-Term Care

Long-term care is one of the most overlooked issues in retirement planning. Nearly 7 million adults over age 65 require long-term care annually[1]. However, most people find it challenging to envision themselves needing this level of daily care. It includes medical and non-medical care for those who have a chronic illness or disability and assists individuals with activities of daily living (ADLs). ADLs are typically broken into six activities:

- Eating
- Walking
- Dressing
- Bathing
- Toileting
- Continence

Unlike general hospital or medical care, most long-term care services are not designed to cure medical conditions. There are several levels of long-term care treatment depending on the level of care needed.

Assisted Living

Provides help with ADLs, medication reminders, meals, and light housekeeping and is designed for people needing daily help but not intense care.

Home Health Care

Intended to be light medical and personal care and is ideal for seniors needing assistance with bathing, dressing, meal preparation, medical reminders, and light housekeeping.

Nursing Home

Designed for those needing continued and complex medical services that may be permanent (Alzheimer's) or short term (surgery recovery).

[1]Eric C. Nordman. The State of Long-Term Care Insurance: The Market, Challenges and Future Innovations, May 2016

How Much Does it Cost?[2]

LTC Service	2017 National Median
Licensed Home Health Aide	$19/Hour
Adult Day Care	$50/Day
Nursing Home (Semi-Private Room)	$238/Day
Nursing Home (Private Room)	$270/Day

Will Medicare Pay for My Coverage?

Medicare is not designed to pay for lengthy long-term care. Medicare limits payment to a skilled nursing or home health care facility. Medicare pays in full for the first 20 days if you are in a skilled nursing facility following a hospital stay. Should a patient continue to have a need for skilled nursing, Medicare may pay a percentage for days 21–100. Medicare will pay nothing toward care after day 100.

Medicaid's Role in Long-Term Care Coverage

Medicaid pays for approximately half of all long-term care expenses nationwide.[3] However, there are significant financial restrictions on qualifying for Medicaid, and these restrictions vary from state to state. The largest restriction is that an individual must spend down nearly all liquid assets in order to qualify. Remember that Medicaid is designed to be a form of welfare for those with no other means of payment for medical service.

Medicaid "Look-Back" Period

There is a 5 year look-back period on the gifting of assets while trying to qualify for Medicaid. Simply giving away assets to family members is not a strategy to qualify for Medicaid.

[2]Genworth Cost of Care Survey, 2017

[3]FFY 2007 Medicaid Statistical Information System (MSIS) Summary File

Long-Term Care Insurance

Long-term care insurance aids in paying the costs associated with long-term care.
When purchasing long-term care coverage, you must carefully weigh the costs and benefits of a policy.
Its also important to consider the costs of burdening loved ones with your care should you be
financially unable to pay for it.

There are a number of key terms to understand when shopping for LTC policies:

Dollar Benefit: Policies are limited to a specified amount per day or per month
(example: $125/day). The higher the coverage, the more expensive a policy.

Duration: Policies for long-term care have a specified period for which they will pay out benefits.
Once the duration period is exhausted, a policy will no longer pay out. Policy durations can
range between 2 and 10 years and may even be unlimited. The longer the duration, the more
costly the policy will be.

Note: The average long-term care stay is 2.4 years, costing $160,000.[4]

Elimination Period: Policies contain an elimination period (30 days, 90 days, 1 year, etc.)
before the insurance coverage begins payment of benefits. The policy holder typically will pay
any costs associated with the stay prior to reaching the elimination period. Shorter elimination
periods will raise the cost of a policy.

COLA: Cost of Living Adjustment (COLA) riders will increase the value of your benefits in line
with a set rate of inflation. COLA riders have a significant cost and value because they allow
benefits to ratchet up with inflation over the course of what may be several decades.

Tax Deductibility of Long-Term Care Insurance

Individuals may be eligible for a tax deduction for a portion of long-term care insurance premiums.
These premiums are classified as medical expenses, and to the extent that they exceed 10% of
your adjusted gross income, they may be deductible.

For self-employed individuals, the deductibility of a policy can be more advantageous. Instead of
being an itemized deduction on Schedule A subject to the 10% of AGI threshold, the premium costs
representing health care are fully deductible as a "self-insured health insurance deduction"
against AGI.

[4]www.ltcfeds.com

When to Buy Long-Term Care Insurance

The longer you wait, the more expensive and challenging it begins to acquire coverage. After age 60, policies can become cost prohibitive. It is also important to remember that nearly 41%[5] of long term care is provided to people under age 65 who need help caring for themselves due to chronic illness or disability. While the ideal time to get a policy is between the ages of 50 and 60, there is a potential value to purchasing a policy earlier and locking in lower rates.

Partnership Program

In an attempt to lower the cost of Medicaid to the states, the Partnership Long Term Care Insurance Program was extended to all states. Owners of a LTC Partnership policy are allowed to protect additional assets in qualifying for Medicaid. For example, if a LTC policy with a benefit value of $250,000 is fully exhausted, then the individual would be allowed to qualify for Medicaid and in doing so still protect $250,000 in assets. Individuals normally would be required to spend down the remaining $250,000 before qualifying for Medicaid.

Self Insuring for Long-Term Care

Given the high expense of long term care facilities, it takes a significant amount of assets to self-insure against the cost. Annual expenses for a stay may likely be $75,000 or higher, and it would take at least $1 million in working assets to self-insure against such an expense.

[5]www.ltcfeds.com

Flexible Spending Accounts (FSAs)

A flexible spending account (FSA), also known as a flexible spending arrangement, is one of a number of tax-advantaged financial accounts that can be set up through a cafeteria plan of an employer. These accounts allow an employee to set aside a portion of his earnings to pay for qualified expenses as established in the cafeteria plan. FSAs are most commonly used for medical expenses but may also be used for dependent care or other expenses. Money deducted from an employee's pre-tax earnings and deposited into an FSA is not subject to payroll taxes, which results in substantial payroll tax savings. One significant disadvantage to using an FSA is that funds not used by the end of the plan year are forfeited by the employee.

RULE OF THUMB

Make sure to spend down your FSA by year end because typically these types of plans forfeit participant balances at the end of the year.

Health Savings Accounts (HSAs)

A health savings account (HSA), is a tax-advantaged medical savings account available to taxpayers who are enrolled in a High Deductible Health Plan (HDHP). The funds contributed to an account are not subject to federal income tax at the time of deposit. Unlike a flexible spending account (FSA), funds roll over and accumulate year to year if not spent.

HSAs are owned by the individual and can be invested in a variety of ways similar to an IRA. HSA funds may be used to pay for qualified medical expenses at any time without federal tax liability or penalty. These accounts are a component of consumer driven health care.

The 2018 annual limitation on tax deductible contributions to a HSA are:

- $3,450 for self-only coverage

- $6,900 for family coverage

- An additional catch-up contribution of $1,000 can be made for individuals over 55 years of age

- You may be allowed a one-time rollover of IRA funds into an HSA up to the annual limit if certain conditions are met.

Casualty Insurance

Casualty insurance is designed to protect assets against damages or total loss. The casualty insurance lines that individuals are most familiar with are automobile insurance and home insurance. In the case of both lines you may not have an option to decline coverage. In most states motorists are required by law to carry automotive liability coverage, and should a home owner carry a mortgage their lender will require home insurance as well.

Just because insurance is legally required does not necessarily mean that the legal minimums for coverage are adequate for your individual situation. For example, if your state only requires $30,000 in coverage for bodily injury, if you were to seriously injure someone else (or yourself) behind the wheel your insurance policy would only cover the first $30,000 in damages leaving you on the hook financially beyond that and potentially in bankruptcy.

The minimum insurance requirement of your mortgage may be inadequate for your needs as well. If you've made improvements to your home the initial policy value may not cover current replacement costs. Also, an important component to home insurance is liability coverage. If you have a property with a pool, a renter, dangerous dog breed or a variety of other risks it is important to make sure your home coverage has the proper risk riders.

Personal Umbrella Insurance

Umbrella insurance refers to a liability insurance policy that protects the assets and future income of a policyholder above and beyond the standard limits of primary policies. It goes into effect only when all underlying policies are totally exhausted. This type of policy shields the insured's assets more broadly than primary coverage.

Typically, an umbrella policy is pure liability coverage over and above the coverage afforded by the regular policy and is sold in increments of one million dollars. The term "umbrella" is used because such insurance covers liability claims from all policies underneath it, such as auto insurance and homeowner's insurance policies. For example, if the insured carries an auto insurance policy with a liability limit of $350,000 and a homeowner's insurance policy with a limit of $250,000, then with a million dollar umbrella, the insured's limits become, in effect, $1,350,000 on an auto liability claim and $1,250,000 on a homeowner's liability claim.

Umbrella insurance provides broad insurance beyond traditional home and auto insurance at an affordable cost. In addition to providing liability coverage above the limits of homeowner's, auto, and boat insurance policies, it can also provide coverage for claims that may be excluded by the primary policies. These may include, but are not limited to:

- Libel   - False arrest
- Slander   - Invasion of privacy

Life Insurance

Life insurance is a contract between the policy owner and the insurer, where the insurer agrees to pay a designated beneficiary a sum of money upon the occurrence of the insured individual's death

It is important to understand your needs for which you are insuring before you begin looking for life insurance.

Life insurance can serve a number of functions:

- Income replacement for surviving spouse

- Education, child care, and other needs of children

- Debt elimination

- Coverage for business owners and key executives

- Legacy for heirs

- Liquidity

- Burial expenses

- Investment

Types of Insurance

Life insurance can be broken into two general types: term and cash value. These different types of insurance meet different insurable needs.

Types of Term Insurance

Level Premium

Premiums and death benefit remain constant for the entire term of the policy.

Annual Renewable

This type of term insurance is renewed annually, usually with a higher premium each year due to an increased risk of death even though death benefits remain the same.

Decreasing Term

Premiums remain constant with this type of insurance but death benefits decrease each year because of the rising chance of death.

When is Term Insurance a Good Option?

– Death benefit coverage is needed for only limited time.

– Permanent insurance coverage is unaffordable.

– There is no need for cash value accumulation or borrowing against the policy.

Term usage examples:

– A newlywed couple purchases a $250,000 home utilizing a 20 year fixed mortgage. A $250,000 decreasing term policy for each individual would be appropriate to pay off mortgage debt.

– A married school teacher with a 15 year-old child is 10 years away from a fully vested pension and taking retirement. A 10 year term policy could be appropriate in this situation to bridge the potential income gap to retirement age and no longer having a dependent child.

RULE OF THUMB

Term insurance is a good form of pure risk management. For working individuals, 5 to 10 times salary is usually appropriate coverage.

Cash Value Life Insurance (Whole, Universal, Variable Universal)

Cash value insurance is generally more expensive than term insurance in the initial years of coverage and will likely cost less than a comparable term policy as you age. In addition to considering costs, it is important to understand what risks you are insuring against before you select the type of insurance to purchase.

Those searching for a more permanent approach to insurance coverage with an interest in building cash value might consider one of the variations of cash value life insurance (whole, universal and variable universal).

Whole Life Insurance

– Level premiums are paid throughout the insured's life.

– In addition to providing mortality coverage, the policy also accumulates cash reserves that are managed by the insurance carrier.

Universal Life Insurance

The distinguishing feature of universal life insurance is that cash values and the death benefit can be modified during the life of the policy.

– Premiums can be offset or eliminated completely by the existing cash value.

– The owner has the ability to make additional premium payments (with limitations) – the difference accumulates in the cash value account.

– Underperforming cash values could endanger a policy, forcing additional premium payments to keep the policy in force.

Variable Universal Life

This type of cash value plan incorporates flexible premiums with the ability to direct investments into sub-accounts within the policy.

– Cash value may be invested in sub-accounts based on the risk tolerance of the policy owner. The variable performance of these accounts will correlate with the cash value and may impact the death benefit.

– Premiums are flexible. Increased contributions to the policy may be invested in available sub-accounts.

– As with universal life, excess cash value in sub-accounts may be used to offset or eliminate premiums.

Other Notes on Cash Value Policies:

– Cash value policies accumulate on a tax deferred and potentially tax-free basis.

– The cash value of a policy generally may be withdrawn (through a policy loan) tax-free. This lowers the death benefit. Interest may be levied and surrender charges may apply.

– Policies may lapse if the cash value can no longer support the death benefit.

Beware Permanent Policies That Aren't So Permanent

Many permanent insurance policies are built on the assumptions that the insurance carrier will have dividend payouts to contract holders. Policies often are constructed under the assumptions that these dividend payments will fund premiums decades in the future. Unfortunately, these dividend payments are not guaranteed, and should an insurance company be unsuccessful at providing significant dividend payouts it could be possible that a permanent policy could skyrocket in cost similar to that of a term contract later in life.

CHAPTER 9:
ESTATE PLANNING

PREPARING FOR RETIREMENT
A COMPREHENSIVE GUIDE TO FINANCIAL PLANNING

ESTATE PLANNING

When we spend a lifetime building wealth, we want to ensure those assets are properly distributed upon our death. Estate planning is the process of anticipating and arranging for the disposal of an estate. Estate planning typically attempts to eliminate uncertainties over the administration of probate and maximize the value of the estate by reducing taxes and other expenses.

Estate planning can become an extremely complicated process, but in its simplest form it is the process of appointing an executor of your estate and naming beneficiaries for your assets. Whether your net worth is $100 million or $10,000, you can benefit from proper estate planning.

Effective estate planning should consider the following:

– Objectives of estate planning

– Will

– Probate

– Powers of attorney (financial and health care)

– Titling of assets

– Beneficiary designations

– Inheriting IRA's and non-qualified assets

– Taxes

– Trusts

Wills

A will is an important legal document in which you provide instructions for the distribution of your estate upon your death and appoint a person to administer your estate.

Your assets will be dispersed upon your death regardless of whether you have a will or not. The choice in the matter is whether you control the distribution of your estate, or if state law makes the decisions for you.

Dying without a will is also referred to as dying "intestate."

Negatives of Dying Without a Will

– You have no control of distribution of assets.

– An administrator of your estate will be appointed for you.

– A guardian will be appointed for any minor children.

– Distant relatives may receive funds meant for charity.

– No assets may transfer to your "significant other" if unmarried.

– There may be unnecessary taxes and legal expenses.

– Assets could go to the state (escheatment).

Advantages of a Will

A will by itself may not create a perfect estate plan, but it does offer the following advantages:

– You select who carries out the terms of your will.

– You indicate beneficiaries.

– You select the guardians for minor children.

– You provide limitations on the distribution of assets.

– You specify assets to be transferred to trusts.

– You guarantee the administration of your estate will be supervised by the courts.

Potential Disadvantages of a Will

– Wills are subject to probate and associated costs.

– Your will can be challenged and creditors can make claims on your estate.

– Probate is public information.

– Assets will not be available to heirs until approval by probate court.

Updating a Will

Wills need to be updated periodically. A change in marital status, birth or death of an intended beneficiary, or a move to a new state should all prompt a review of your will.

Required Elements of a Will

The requirements for a valid will are different from state to state, but most state statutes have these basic requirements:

- State your name.

- It was executed with testamentary intent (dying wishes).

- At the time the will was drawn and executed, you had the ability to understand what is in the will (testamentary capacity).

- It was executed without undue influence, duress, or the like.

- It was duly executed to be in compliance with statutory requirements (signatures, witnesses, etc.).

Additional Elements of a Will

- Description of assets

- Names of spouse, children, and other beneficiaries such as charities or friends

- Alternate beneficiaries

- Specific gifts, such as an auto or residence

- Establishment of trusts, if desired

- Cancellation of debts owed to you, if desired

- Name of an executor to manage the estate

- Name of a guardian for minor children

- Name of an alternative guardian, in case your first choice is unable or unwilling to act

Naming an Executor

An executor is the person who oversees the distribution of your assets in accordance to your will. If no executor is named in a will, a probate judge will appoint one. Responsibilities often undertaken by an executor include:

- Paying valid creditors

- Paying taxes

- Notifying Social Security and other agencies and companies of the death

- Canceling credit cards, magazine subscriptions, etc.

- Identifying assets of the estate

- Distributing assets according to the will

Because of the important duties of an executor, you should take great care with the appointment. An attorney or trust company can be appointed should you have difficulty appointing an individual.

RULE OF THUMB

Review your estate planning documents every 5 years or after major life changes to ensure they are up to date with your wishes.

Understanding Probate

Probate is the legal process of administering the estate of a deceased person by resolving all claims and distributing the deceased person's property under a valid will. The courts decide the validity of a decedent's will. The probate process interprets the instructions of the deceased, officially appoints the executor as the personal representative of the estate, and adjudicates the interests of heirs and other parties who may have claims against the estate.

The Steps of Probate

– Determining the validity of a decedent's will

– Taking inventory and appraisal of the decedent's property

– Paying claims from creditors as well as potential taxes and estate expenses

– Distributing the remaining property as the will (or intestate law) describes

– Handling challenges

Probated Assets

– Individually owned (non-qualified) assets

– Assets with beneficiary listed as "estate"

– Community property

– Property owned as tenants in common

Assets Bypassing Probate

– Joint tenancy with rights of survivorship (JTWROS)

– Revocable living trusts

– Transfer-on-death (TOD) accounts

– Assets with a beneficiary designated

– Property conveyed by deeds of title

Want more privacy? Probated wills are subject to public inspection. If this is a problematic, then you may want to consider titling assets into a revocable living trust which will shield your assets from public inspection.

Powers of Attorney

A Power of Attorney (POA) is a legal document authorizing one to act on someone else's behalf in a legal or business matter. The person authorizing the other to act is the principal, grantor, or donor (of the power), and the one authorized to act is the agent or attorney-in-fact.

A Durable Power of Attorney is a useful form for anyone to have in place. It can go into effect immediately (or "spring" upon incompetence) and remains in effect even after an individual is no longer able to manage his financial affairs. Court proceedings typically will decide who will manage financials going forward if no such power of attorney is in place.

An agent or attorney-in-fact is required to act in the best interest of the principal (fiduciary capacity). This includes maintaining accurate records and separating personal assets from those related to the power of attorney.

Potential Roles of an Agent

- Pay everyday expenses and bills
- Collect benefits like Social Security, Medicare, and pensions
- Invest your money in stocks, bonds, and mutual funds
- Maintain and transact real estate and other property
- File and pay taxes
- Operate a business

The role of the agent is a tremendous responsibility. When considering a durable power of attorney for your finances, keep in mind your agent should be:

- Competent
- Trustworthy
- Willing to assume responsibility
- Accessible

Requirements for a properly executed POA differ from state to state. Documents usually have to be notarized, and they may be required to be recorded in your local court house. As long as the grantor is competent, a POA can be revoked at any time.

Remember: POA documents expire when you do! Don't expect to use one after the grantor is deceased.

Health Care Power of Attorney

A health care power of attorney allows you to direct your agent to make health care decisions in the case of your incapacitation.

Health Care Declaration/Living Will

The health care declaration, often called your living will, details the type of care you desire in the event of incapacitation. The health care power of attorney can be used to grant the authority to oversee your wishes as set forth in your health care declaration as well as the power to make other necessary decisions about health care matters. One of the most important decisions you must make in a living will is the extent to which you wish your life be extended "artificially."

Some states combine the health care power of attorney and living will into one form called the Advance Health Care Directive.

RULE OF THUMB

Beware of placing more than 2 people in charge of your living will. Having 3 people or more can make it difficult to reach a consensus about your care.

Different Titles of Assets

Title represents ownership of a given asset and also dictates how the asset will pass at the owner's death. Depending on the type of asset, you may have a variety of choices in titling assets.

Joint Tenants with Rights of Survivorship (JTWROS)

In joint tenancy, an asset is owned by two or more people while each tenant has an equal right to the assets. At the death of a co-owner, assets pass directly to the other joint tenant(s) and the assets are not subject to probate in the deceased estate. JTWROS provides for a quick and efficient transfer of title that preempts your will.

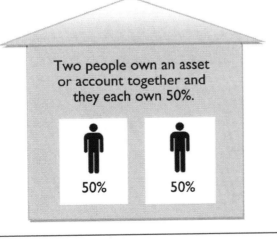

Two people own an asset or account together and they each own 50%.

50%   50%

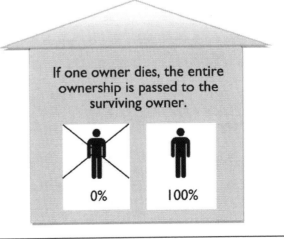

If one owner dies, the entire ownership is passed to the surviving owner.

0%   100%

Tenancy by the Entirety

Tenancy by the entirety is a form of ownership created by a conveyance from spouse to spouse, and is only available to married couples. Similar to joint tenancy, the parties must acquire property interest through one title at the same time. Equal rights of possession and equal interest in the property are requirements of tenancy by the entirety.

The main difference between tenancy by the entirety and joint tenancy is that the tenants can not singularly transact the property. In traditional joint tenancy if one joint tenant conveys interest in the property, that interest is conveyed thus destroying the joint tenancy. However, in tenancy by the entirety, each tenant owns the entire estate. This relationship means that neither tenant can deal with the property independently of the other. The primary advantage of this relationship is that a creditor of one party cannot enforce liens against joint property held in tenancy by entirety.

Joint tenancy by the entirety is only available in certain states and may be restricted to only real estate.

Tenancy in Common (TIC)

Tenancy in common allows for joint owners to have unequal stakes in an asset. Additionally, each owner's stake passes in accordance with his will, not automatically to the other joint owners.

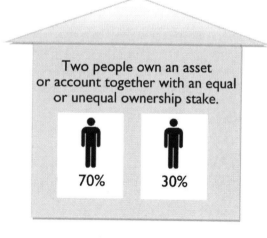

Two people own an asset or account together with an equal or unequal ownership stake.

70% 30%

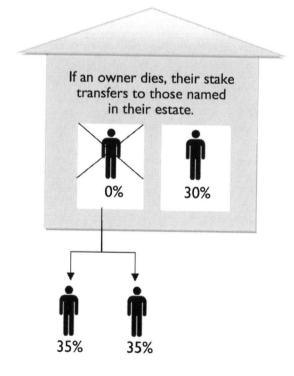

If an owner dies, their stake transfers to those named in their estate.

0% 30%

35% 35%

Community Property

In a community property jurisdiction, most property acquired during the marriage (except for gifts or inheritances) is owned jointly by both spouses and is divided upon divorce, annulment, or death. The community property system is usually justified by the idea that both spouses equally created and contributed to the operation and assets of a family unit.

Community property states include:

Arizona, California, Idaho, Louisiana, Nevada, New Mexico, Texas, Washington, and Wisconsin

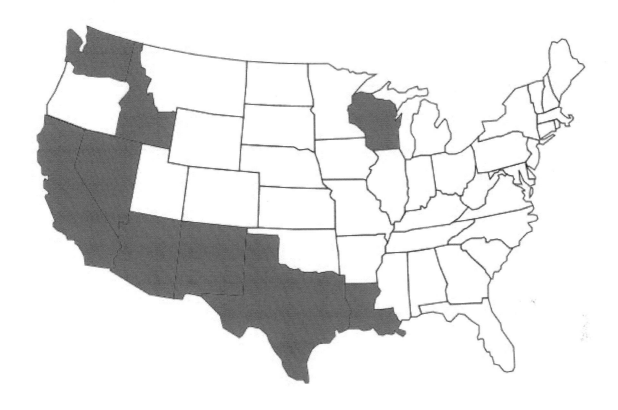

Transfer-on-Death (TOD)

Provisions exist to arrange for direct transfer upon death, bypassing the estate and probate. Beneficiaries may be designated via transfer-on-death (TOD) provisions for certain types of accounts. Beneficiaries receive assets upon the owner's death but hold no other account holder rights until that point. A brokerage firm or bank may not allow the use of TOD registration.

Beneficiaries

Many types of assets transfer through beneficiary designations rather than your will, estate, or trusts. Assets that require beneficiary designations include retirement plans and insurance products. In many instances you can name primary and contingent beneficiaries.

Reasons to Update Beneficiaries:

- – To ensure assets pass to the correct parties
- – To allow designated assets to bypass the probate process
- – To potentially continue tax-deferred or tax-free growth in retirement accounts that may be lost if the assets are probated.

RULE OF THUMB

Be cautious of naming minor children or grandchildren as beneficiaries. A court may need to appoint a financial guardian to receive the assets on their behalf.

Inheriting an IRA

Individuals designated as a beneficiary of an IRA will have several distribution options upon inheriting an IRA. The factors affecting options available are your relationship to the deceased IRA owner and whether the IRA owner passed away before or after beginning required minimum distributions (age 70 ½).

Spousal Beneficiary Options

1. Roll assets to their own IRA

The spouse will be able to continue the tax-deferral and will start taking required minimum distributions (RMDs) based on that person's own life expectancy once he reaches age 70 1/2.

2. Establish an Inherited IRA

The spouse will be able to continue the tax-deferral and will begin RMDs the year the deceased would have reached age 70 1/2. If the deceased was over 70 1/2, the surviving older spouse may have smaller RMDs based on the life expectancy of the original account owner.

3. Exercise the 5-Year Rule

If the deceased spouse had not begun taking RMDs, the surviving spouse may elect to utilize the 5-year rule. This option is available only if the account owner dies before the required beginning date for receiving RMDs. Distributions can be taken in any amount or frequency as long as the account is depleted by December 31st of the fifth year following the account owner's death.

4. Take a Lump Sum Payment

All IRA beneficiaries can elect to receive assets as a lump sum. The 10% early withdrawal penalty for distributions prior to the age of 59 1/2 does not apply, but distributions will be subject to federal and state income taxes.

Non-Spousal IRA Beneficiary Options

A non-spouse IRA beneficiary also has the options of utilizing the 5-year rule or taking a lump sum payment. Additionally, a non-spouse beneficiary may transfer the assets to an inherited IRA to continue the potential tax-deferred growth of assets.

If the deceased had not begun RMDs, the non-spouse beneficiary will take required minimum distributions over that person's own life expectancy.

If the deceased had begun RMDs, required distributions can be taken over the longer of the beneficiary's life expectancy or the remaining single life expectancy of the deceased account owner.

Note: Distributions must begin by December 31st of the following year of the account owner's death.

"Stretch" IRA

The stretch IRA strategy simply implies taking the required minimum distributions from the account each year at its latest point to avoid any type of penalty. This allows the remaining assets to continue growing tax-deferred as long as possible, thus leaving a maximized amount which will eventually pass to your beneficiaries.

In order to "force" a beneficiary to take only required minimum distributions upon your death, further estate planning may be needed.

Step-Up in Cost Basis

Upon inheriting a non-qualified asset, individuals will receive a "step-up in cost basis". The cost basis of an asset is adjusted (up or down) to reflect the market price at the time of inheritance (decedent's date of death).

Example: You inherit your parent's house that was purchased 30 years ago for $75,000. Today, the home's market value is $225,000. Your cost basis will be $225,000; thus, you will avoid paying capital gains taxes on $150,000 of appreciation.

RULE OF THUMB

Distribute assets with large unrealized gains upon your death so that your beneficiaries receive a step-up in cost basis. By doing so you will not pay capital gains taxes on the sale during your lifetime, and your beneficiaries will recognize fewer gains upon the subsequent sale.

Federal Estate Taxes

Estate taxes are imposed upon the fair market value of a decedent's estate. However, only a small percentage of individuals will actually owe estate tax because estate taxes are due only on estates that exceed the lifetime exemption amount. According to the IRS, only about 3,700 estates, or 0.12% of the total, are expected to owe a federal estate tax in 2017.

The exemption amount has increased steadily over the past decade. Recent legislation has increased the lifetime exemption to $11.2 million per person, which is also indexed for inflation going forward.

Year	Exemption	Top Tax Rate	Year	Exemption	Top Tax Rate
2003	$1,000,000	49%	2011	$5,000,000	35%
2004	$1,500,000	48%	2012	$5,120,000	35%
2005	$1,500,000	47%	2013	$5,250,000	40%
2006	$2,000,000	46%	2014	$5,340,000	40%
2007	$2,000,000	45%	2015	$5,430,000	40%
2008	$2,000,000	45%	2016	$5,450,000	40%
2009	$3,500,000	45%	2017	$5,490,000	40%
2010	$5,000,000 or $0	35% or 0%	2018	$11,200,000	40%

Unlimited Marital Deduction

An unlimited amount of assets can be transferred tax-free to a surviving spouse upon a decedent's death. Note that some restrictions apply for non-US citizen spouses.

Portability Provision

In the past, if you left all your assets to a spouse, you would lose your applicable exclusion. However, recent legislation has provided a "portability" provision whereby the executor of a deceased spouse's estate may transfer any unused exemption to the surviving spouse (only available for decedents dying after December 2010). This means a total of two times the exemption from federal estate tax may be available to a surviving spouse. Portability simplifies estate planning since it no longer requires advanced estate planning techniques to ensure that both spouses are properly utilizing the full applicable exclusion amount. Note that the portability will be lost if the surviving spouse remarries. Also, it does not apply to the generation skipping transfer tax exclusion amount.

[1]Tax Policy Center, Center for Disease Control

State Estate Tax

Despite the generous increase in the federal estate tax exemption and addition of the portability provision in 2011, it is important to note that 18 states and Washington, D.C. impose their own estate or inheritance taxes. Thus, wealthy families could still face estate planning issues imposed by their respective state.

Gifting

One of the simplest ways to lower your taxable estate is to gift assets to relatives and friends during your lifetime. Beneficiaries are not taxed on the receipt of a gift, but the donor will be subject to tax on the fair market value of the gift that exceeds the annual exclusion amount. The 2018 gift tax annual exclusion amount (the amount you can gift in a year tax-free) is $15,000 per donor per donee, meaning a couple can gift $30,000 annually to any individual gift tax-free. A gift tax return (Form 709) must be filed if gifts are in excess of the annual exclusion amount.

Gifts in excess of the annual exclusion amount will deplete the amount of the lifetime applicable exclusion available at death. In other words, the exemption is the total that can be transferred tax-free during life and at death.

As noted previously, gift recipients do not need to pay income taxes on the receipt of gifts. The donor's original cost basis and holding period of the gift will transfer with the gift to the donee. Unlike assets inherited at death, no step-up in cost basis is given on gifted assets.

Note: Some states may impose additional gift taxes. Also, gifts made within 3 years of death must be added back to a decedent's gross estate.

Generation Skipping Tax (GST)

Individuals with large sums of wealth may find it attractive to pass assets to grandchildren and subsequent generations. To avoid the loss of tax revenue for these types of gifts that bypass generations, Uncle Sam has imposed a generation skipping transfer tax (GST). GST is an additional tax that is imposed on transfers during life and at death on gifts made to a recipient who is at least two generations younger than the donor or decedent (e.g., grandchildren). For 2018, there is a $11.2 million exemption from GST per individual. This exemption is available for gifts and transfers at death and allows for this amount to be passed to future generations or a dynasty trust in order to minimize taxation.

Trusts

A trust is a relationship between three parties whereby property is transferred to be held by another party for the benefit of a third party. A trust can have conditions on the manner in which assets are distributed. While there are many misconceptions of trusts, they have a variety of uses within family and estate planning.

Uses of a Trust:

- The ability to place conditions on how and when assets will be distributed.

- Potential reduction of estate and gift taxes.

- Avoidance of additional cost and publicity of probate.

- Protection from claims of creditors or lawsuits.

- Protection of assets for minors or financially irresponsible beneficiaries.

Elements of a Trust Include:

- **Trust Agreement:** A written, legal document created by the grantor that specifies terms of the trust.

- **Trust Property (corpus or principal)**: The property funding the trust.

- **Grantor or Trustor:** The person that creates and funds the trust.

- **Trustee:** The party who holds legal title to the property placed in the trust and who generally manages and distributes income according to terms of the trust. Individuals or institutions may serve as trustees.

- **Beneficiary:** The party for whose benefit the trust is created and who will receive benefits of income and/or principal according to the terms in the trust.

Common Types of Trusts

- Revocable living trust

- Irrevocable trust

- Irrevocable life insurance trust

- Testamentary trust (takes effect after death)

- Credit shelter trust or A-B trust

- Charitable trust

Revocable Living Trusts

Revocable living trusts can be used in many capacities as a substitute for a will and are effective in avoiding the costs and publicity of probate. Most grantors list themselves as trustee and beneficiary of their living trust, which enables them to retain all rights to the assets titled to the trust.

Features of revocable living trusts:

- Grantor has flexibility to terminate the trust and change the terms, trustee(s), and beneficiaries.
- The trust becomes irrevocable upon the grantor's death, at which point, the trust terminates with the trust assets being distributed or continuing for a specified time.
- The transfer of property to the trust does not constitute a taxable gift since the grantor retains equitable title, making the gift incomplete for tax purposes.
- All income earned by a revocable trust is taxable to the grantor at individual income tax rates.
- Probate is avoided (if all assets are included in the trust).
- The trust is included in your taxable estate at death.
- The trust does not save income or estate taxes, and assets within the trust are not protected from creditors.

Don't Forget: After creating an revocable trust, remember to title assets properly into the trust.

Irrevocable Trusts

Irrevocable trusts are legal entities that hold assets for beneficiaries. Since this type of trust is irrevocable, any assets donated cannot be retrieved and typically the parties and terms of the trust cannot be changed.

Because the grantor releases equitable and legal title to assets donated to a irrevocable trust, a contribution to the trust is considered a completed gift for tax purposes. This means gift taxes may be due on any assets passing into a irrevocable trust, but at death these assets will not be part of the deceased taxable estate.

Irrevocable Life Insurance Trust (ILIT)

One practical use of irrevocable trusts in estate planning is the use of the trust in combination with life insurance. Typically the death benefit of a life insurance policy is received by a beneficiary income tax free. However, life insurance proceeds may be subject to estate tax. A properly built irrevocable life insurance trust (ILIT) may be utilized to protect life insurance proceeds from estate taxes, probate, and creditors.

While the use of an ILIT may be an effective strategy for protecting assets from estate taxes, the irrevocable nature of the trust results in the grantor losing the ability to change beneficiaries in the future. The creation of an ILIT is complicated, and professional help should be sought by anyone initiating this strategy.

Testamentary Trust

Testamentary trusts are created in accordance with instructions contained within a decedent's will. Testamentary trusts do not become active until the grantor passes away, and the grantor keeps control during his lifetime. The assets will be included in the grantor's estate and they will be probated before passing into the testamentary trust.

Don't Forget: A testamentary trust is subject to probate.

Credit Shelter or A-B Trust

The A-B trust is an estate planning tool that allows both spouses to utilize the applicable exclusion amount ($11,100,000 for 2018). This type of trust is referred to as a credit shelter trust, family exclusion trust, or bypass trust. It is generally created by will (or living trust) and becomes irrevocable upon the grantor's death. Before the portability of the applicable exclusion amount was enacted, the A-B trust was one of the most efficient means of maximizing the amount a couple could shelter from estate taxes.

Traditionally, by leaving all assets directly to a surviving spouse, the first spouse to die wasted his exclusion amount. The A-B trust was designed to reduce estate taxes upon the death of the second spouse.

How it works:

- At the death of the first spouse, the decedent's estate is split into two separate trusts: Trust A is funded up to the applicable exclusion amount (currently $5,340,000), ensuring that the applicable exclusion amount is fully utilized. The remaining estate assets are used to fund trust B, which will benefit the surviving spouse.

- Property in Trust A will go to the named beneficiaries. However, the surviving spouse usually retains the right to use the property in Trust A for the remainder of his or her lifetime. Principal from Trust A may also be accessed in certain circumstances for a surviving spouse's health and support needs.

- On the death of the second spouse, both applicable exclusion amounts have been utilized, and the final beneficiaries receive the property of both Trusts A and B. Additionally, if the assets in Trust A have appreciated in value, the increase is not subject to estate taxation. Assets expected to greatly increase in value are excellent subjects for placement in Trust A.

- Trust B property is not considered part of the second spouse's estate for estate tax purposes. It "bypasses" the survivor's estate at his or her death.

Charitable Trusts

Assets can be gifted to a charity either before or after death through the use of a charitable trust. In addition to benefiting a charity or foundation, a charitable trust can potentially reduce the size of your estate (and estate taxes) and income taxes.

Charitable Remainder Trust (CRT)

Establishing a Charitable Remainder Trust (CRT) allows a grantor to provide a gift to a qualifying charity while creating an income stream for a beneficiary (the grantor or any other beneficiary). The income stream can be for the life of the beneficiary or for a stated term of years. At the end of the income generating period, the remainder interest passes to the qualified charity.

Benefits

- The grantor or beneficiary may receive an income stream for life.
- Donated assets avoid capital gains taxation.
- An income tax deduction is available in the year of the gift for the present value of the remainder interest.
- You may lower the total value of your estate as the donated assets are removed.
- You retain some control over how the assets are invested.
- You may have the ability to change the qualified charities.

Charitable Lead Trust (CLT)

A Charitable Lead Trust works in reverse of the Remainder Trust, as the charity receives the income while the beneficiaries receive the remainder after a specified period of time. The donor may potentially claim a charitable income tax deduction for making the gift.

Do it Yourself Estate Planning

Many people wonder if the wills sold online are fully legal—The answer is yes. There are a number of reputable resources online where you can purchase a variety of legal documents. However, like any do-it-yourself project, there are caveats. First of all, estate planning laws can vary from state to state, and the vendor you purchase documents from online may only be selling a generic document. Secondly, there are many fine and subtle details to proper estate planning. While the hammer and saw at the hardware store are very capable of building a house, those tools in unskilled hands won't build a quality home. Keep in mind that more complex estate planning needs require the skill of an attorney. Finally, laws are constantly changing, and you should ensure that all your legal documents are up-to-date so you can ensure your assets pass efficiently to the beneficiary of your choosing.

Summary

Retirement and financial planning are continuous processes. Unfortunately the shelf life of this text is limited because many of the laws and rules covered can and will be drastically changed with the stroke of a pen in the years to come. For this reason, it is vital to consistently review your plans in order to keep them up-to-date and work with financial professionals who are tracking these changes.

Remember, the stock market, Congress, and the economy should not dictate your financial goals. Put yourself in charge of your financial plan and take control of your future.

APPENDIX:

FINANCIAL PLANNING FORMS

PREPARING FOR RETIREMENT

A Comprehensive Guide to Financial Planning

Preparing for Retirement
A Comprehensive Guide to Financial Planning

PERSONAL INFORMATION

CONTACT INFORMATION

Individual 1

Full name: _____

Date of Birth: _____

Social Security #: _____ - _____ - _____

Individual 2

Full name: _____

Date of Birth: _____

Social Security #: _____ - _____ - _____

ADDRESS & EMPLOYMENT INFORMATION

Individual 1

Email: _____

Phone: _____

Address: _____

City: _____

State: _____ Zip: _____

Individual 2

Email: _____

Phone: _____

Address: _____

City: _____

State: _____ Zip: _____

EMPLOYMENT

Individual 1

Employer: _____

Job Title: _____

Phone: _____

Address: _____

City: _____

State: _____ Zip: _____

Employment Period: _____

Individual 2

Employer: _____

Job Title: _____

Phone: _____

Address: _____

City: _____

State: _____ Zip: _____

Employment Period: _____

PROFESSIONAL SERVICES

CPA/Tax Software: _____

Estate Attorney: _____

Insurance Agent: _____

Banking: _____

Investment Advisor/Firm: _____

PENSION, EARNED INCOME & SOCIAL SECURITY

DEFINED PENSION INFORMATION

Defined Pension Information: Include information on pensions that provide an annual income level (e.g., military pension, state pension)

	Individual 1 Pension 1	Pension 2	Individual 2 Pension 1	Pension 2
Anticipated annual amount:	$_____	$_____	$_____	$_____
Starting age:	_____	_____	_____	_____
Increase rate before retirement:	_____%	_____%	_____%	_____%
Increase rate after retirement:	_____%	_____%	_____%	_____%
Survivor benefit (%):	_____%	_____%	_____%	_____%

	Individual 1	Individual 2
EARNED INCOME		
Earned income now:	$_____	_____
SOCIAL SECURITY		
Age to start benefit:	_____	_____
Annual increase rate:	_____%	_____%
Estimated or current annual benefit:	$_____	$_____

ESTATE

Check the box if you have any of the following:

	Individual 1	Individual 2
Will	☐	☐
Revocable Living Trust	☐	☐
Martial Trust Provisions	☐	☐
Credit Shelter Trust Provisions	☐	☐
Health Care Power of Attorney	☐	☐
Irrevocable Life Insurance Trust	☐	☐
Durable General Power of Attorney	☐	☐
Living Will	☐	☐
Executor	☐	☐

INSURANCE

INSURANCE INFORMATION

You may need to review your insurance policies in order to get this information.

	Individual 1	Individual 2
Permanent life insurance:	$ _____	$ _____
Term life insurance:	$ _____	$ _____
Cash values (less loans):	$ _____	$ _____
Long-term care insurance:	$ _____	$ _____
Car coverage:	$ _____	$ _____
Umbrella coverage:	$ _____	$ _____

EDUCATION FUNDING

CHILDREN'S EDUCATION AND FUND EXPENSES

Child's Name	Age	Age to start college	Cost per year*	# of years	Current college fund
_____	____	_____	$ _____	_____	$ _____
_____	____	_____	$ _____	_____	$ _____
_____	____	_____	$ _____	_____	$ _____
_____	____	_____	$ _____	_____	$ _____
_____	____	_____	$ _____	_____	$ _____
_____	____	_____	$ _____	_____	$ _____
_____	____	_____	$ _____	_____	$ _____
_____	____	_____	$ _____	_____	$ _____

Inflation rate to use for college planner: _____ %

Rate of return on college funds: _____ %

College fund account types (529, UGMA, Etc.): _____

*In today's dollars

ASSETS

List capital assets including banking accounts, investment accounts, stocks, bonds, mutual funds, business interests and other financial assets.

No.	Asset name	Current value*	Annual Additions	Account description (i.e. stock, 401k, bank account, etc)	Owner
1	_____	$ _____	$ _____	_____	_____
2	_____	$ _____	$ _____	_____	_____
3	_____	$ _____	$ _____	_____	_____
4	_____	$ _____	$ _____	_____	_____
5	_____	$ _____	$ _____	_____	_____
6	_____	$ _____	$ _____	_____	_____
7	_____	$ _____	$ _____	_____	_____
8	_____	$ _____	$ _____	_____	_____
9	_____	$ _____	$ _____	_____	_____
10	_____	$ _____	$ _____	_____	_____
11	_____	$ _____	$ _____	_____	_____
12	_____	$ _____	$ _____	_____	_____
13	_____	$ _____	$ _____	_____	_____
14	_____	$ _____	$ _____	_____	_____
15	_____	$ _____	$ _____	_____	_____

ADDITIONAL ASSETS/DEBTS

Other Asset Values		Owner	Other Debts/Liabilities		Owner
Residence value:	$_____	_____	Residence mortgage:	$_____	_____
Personal property:	$_____	_____	Credit card balances:	$_____	_____
Autos:	$_____	_____	Autos loans:	$_____	_____
Boats, RVs, etc:	$_____	_____	Boats, RVs, etc. loans:	$_____	_____
Other assets:	$_____	_____	Other Loans:	$_____	_____

TAXES

CURRENT TAXES

Last Year AGI: $ _____

Effective (Avg.) Tax Rate: _____ %

FUTURE TAXES

Estimate present and post-retirement effective income tax rates.

Effective income tax rate before retirement: _____ %

Effective income tax rate after retirement: _____ %

INVESTMENT GAINS/LOSSES

Unrealized Investment Gains (if any): $ _____

Carryover Losses (if any): $ _____

PREPARING FOR RETIREMENT
A COMPREHENSIVE GUIDE TO FINANCIAL PLANNING

BUDGET CALCULATION WORKSHEET

EXPENSES

Estimate annual figures for expenses related to shelter, food, clothing, transportation, insurance, loans, etc. Do not include taxes.

Annual Living Expenses (today's dollars)

Now: $ _____

Current Surviving Household: $ _____

During Retirement: $ _____

Single Retiree Survivor: $ _____

Annual inflation rates for living expenses

Before Retirement: _____ %

Surviving Household: _____ %

During Retirement: _____ %

Single Retiree Survivor: _____ %

SPECIAL INCOME/EXPENSES

Description	Annual amount	Increase rate	Starting year	# of years	Priority
_____	$ _____	_____ %	_____	_____	_____
_____	$ _____	_____ %	_____	_____	_____
_____	$ _____	_____ %	_____	_____	_____
_____	$ _____	_____ %	_____	_____	_____
_____	$ _____	_____ %	_____	_____	_____
_____	$ _____	_____ %	_____	_____	_____
_____	$ _____	_____ %	_____	_____	_____
_____	$ _____	_____ %	_____	_____	_____
_____	$ _____	_____ %	_____	_____	_____
_____	$ _____	_____ %	_____	_____	_____
_____	$ _____	_____ %	_____	_____	_____
_____	$ _____	_____ %	_____	_____	_____

PREPARING FOR RETIREMENT
A COMPREHENSIVE GUIDE TO FINANCIAL PLANNING

EXPENSE WORKSHEET – ESTIMATED MONTHLY EXPENSES

ITEM	NOW	RETIREMENT	SURVIVOR NOW	SURVIVOR RETIREMENT
RENT OR LEASE PAYMENT				
FOOD & HOUSEHOLD INCIDENTALS				
UTILITIES, TELEPHONE				
AUTO OPERATING AND MAINTENANCE				
CLOTHING AND PERSONAL ITEMS				
PROPERTY IMPROVEMENT & UPKEEP				
DOMESTIC HELP, BABYSITTING				
PROPERTY TAXES				
ENTERTAINMENT & VACATIONS				
CHARITABLE CONTRIBUTIONS				
CHILDCARE				
ALIMONY, CHILD SUPPORT				
BOOKS, PAPERS, SUBSCRIPTIONS				
HOME FURNISHINGS				
GIFTS, BIRTHDAYS				
MEDICAL EXPENSES				
OTHER EXPENSES				
MORTGAGE PAYMENT				
AUTO LOAN PAYMENT				
BOAT & RV PAYMENTS				
CREDIT CARD PAYMENTS				
OTHER LOAN PAYMENTS				
LIFE INSURANCE PREMIUMS				
MEDICAL INSURANCE PREMIUMS				
AUTO INSURANCE PREMIUMS				
HOUSE INSURANCE PREMIUMS				
OTHER INSURANCE PREMIUMS				

PREPARING FOR RETIREMENT
A COMPREHENSIVE GUIDE TO FINANCIAL PLANNING

RISK ASSESSMENT QUESTIONNAIRE

1. When making a long-term investment, I plan on holding the investment for:

    1. ☐ 1-2 Years

    2. ☐ 2-5 Years

    3. ☐ 5-10 Years

    4. ☐ 10+ Years

2. In 2008, stocks lost over 30% in 3 months. If I lost 30% in 3 months, I would:

    1. ☐ Sell all remaining investment

    2. ☐ Sell a portion of investment

    3. ☐ Hold investment and make no change

    4. ☐ Buy more of the investment

3. Generally, I prefer investments with little fluctuation and will accept a lower rate of return for it.

    1. ☐ Strongly Agree

    2. ☐ Slightly Agree

    3. ☐ Slightly Disagree

    4. ☐ Strongly Disagree

4. I would invest in a stock solely based on a brief conversation with friend or co-worker.

    1. ☐ Strongly Disagree

    2. ☐ Slightly Disagree

    3. ☐ Slightly Agree

    4. ☐ Strongly Agree

5. The chart below shows the greatest 1 year gain on 3 different hypothetical investments of $10,000. Given the potential gain or loss in any 1 year, I would invest my money in:

    1. ☐ A

    2. ☐ B

    3. ☐ C

RISK ASSESSMENT QUESTIONNAIRE

6. My current and future income sources are (salary, pension, investment income, etc.):

   1. ☐ Very unstable

   2. ☐ Unstable

   3. ☐ Stable

   4. ☐ Very stable

7. During a market correction (stocks down 10% or more), I check my account balance:

   1. ☐ Several times a day

   2. ☐ Once a day

   3. ☐ Once a week

   4. ☐ Once a month or less

8. My current investment allocation is:

   1. ☐ I don't know

   2. ☐ Mostly low risk assets like bonds/CDs/cash

   3. ☐ Well diversified between stocks and bonds/CDs/cash

   4. ☐ Mostly stocks or stock mutual funds

SCORING

Look at the number beside each answer and sum all numbers together for your total score.

My Score: _____

Low Risk Investor:	12 Points or Lower
Moderate Risk Investor:	12 to 23 Points
Aggressive Risk Investor:	24 Points or Higher

PREPARING FOR RETIREMENT
A COMPREHENSIVE GUIDE TO FINANCIAL PLANNING

INDEX

PREPARING FOR RETIREMENT
A COMPREHENSIVE GUIDE TO FINANCIAL PLANNING

INDEX

PREPARING FOR RETIREMENT
A COMPREHENSIVE GUIDE TO FINANCIAL PLANNING

INDEX